Self-Financed Candidates
in Congressional Elections

CONTEMPORARY POLITICAL AND SOCIAL ISSUES

Alan Wolfe, Series Editor

Contemporary Political and Social Issues provides a forum in which social scientists and seasoned observers of the political scene use their expertise to comment on issues of contemporary importance in American politics, including immigration, affirmative action, religious conflict, gay rights, welfare reform, and globalization.

Self-Financed Candidates in Congressional Elections

JENNIFER A. STEEN

THE UNIVERSITY OF MICHIGAN PRESS

ANN ARBOR

Copyright © by the University of Michigan 2006
All rights reserved
Published in the United States of America by
The University of Michigan Press
Manufactured in the United States of America
♾ Printed on acid-free paper

2009   2008   2007   2006   4   3   2   1

A CIP catalog record for this book is available from the British Library.

Library of Congress Cataloging-in-Publication Data

Steen, Jennifer A.
Self-financed candidates in congressional elections / Jennifer A. Steen.
    p.   cm. — (Contemporary political and social issues)
Includes bibliographical references and index.
ISBN-13: 978-0-472-09903-0 (cloth : alk. paper)
ISBN-10: 0-472-09903-5 (cloth : alk. paper)
ISBN-13: 978-0-472-06903-3 (pbk. : alk. paper)
ISBN-10: 0-472-06903-9 (pbk. : alk. paper)
1. Self-financed political candidates—United States.   2. Campaign funds—United States.
3. Campaign funds—United States—Statistics.   4. United States. Congress—Elections.
I. Title.   II. Series.

JK1991.S72   2006
324.7′8′0973—dc22   2005022348

Contents

Acknowledgments

I WOULD LIKE TO ACKNOWLEDGE a few individuals and organizations who supported my campaign to become a published author. Like any good politician let me first acknowledge my campaign contributors. My grandparents, David and Merna Scott, generously picked up the bulk of the tab for my graduate education, and I am sorry they did not live to see me earn my Ph.D. and turn my dissertation into this book. I am also grateful for dissertation fellowships from the Political Science department at the University of California, Berkeley, and for a research fellowship from the Governmental Studies department at the Brookings Institution. The Institute of Governmental Studies at Berkeley gave me several grants to fund data collection and travel between Berkeley and Washington, D.C. At Boston College I received funding for data collection and research assistance to update the manuscript.

My campaign also benefited from a large network of volunteers. Those who read and commented on iterations of the entire manuscript include Henry Brady, Bruce Cain, Marc Landy, Nelson Polsby, Susan Rasky, and Kay Schlozman. I must also thank Bruce and Nelson for throwing the weight of the Institute of Governmental Studies behind me. IGS was my home on the Berkeley campus, where I enjoyed office space, computer equipment, a wonderful library, and several opportunities to present pieces of my research. Many other individuals have provided helpful comments on sections of the manuscript, including Paul Herrnson, Gary Jacobson, Michael Malbin, and Tom Mann, as well as the anonymous reviewers for the University of Michigan Press.

Student "interns" from Boston College helped me finish the book and learned about political science research while doing so. Elizabeth

Kabacinski and Lauren Daniel were the enthusiastic and resourceful BC undergraduates who helped me track down key examples and citations. Tobin Craig, a doctoral student at BC, was especially helpful in sifting through the *Congressional Record*. Caitlin O'Donnell and Richard Martin also contributed to the data collection.

On the campaign trail I made several public appearances where seminar participants and conference attendees often offered fresh ideas. I thank my hosts at Boston College (where my future colleagues were especially engaging), the University of Maryland, Wellesley College, the Brennan Center for Justice at NYU, the Brookings Institution, and UC Berkeley.

It may be a stretch to liken the University of Michigan Press to national party headquarters, but I'm enjoying the campaign metaphor too much not to! Many thanks to Alan Wolfe, editor of the series in which this book appears and my colleague at BC, who recruited me to run on the UM Press line. I am also grateful to Boss Jim Reische, particularly for his patience.

Finally, I would especially like to thank the two gentlemen of my kitchen cabinet. Raymond E. Wolfinger, my dissertation adviser, commented on multiple drafts of this manuscript and its component chapters. I am grateful for the careful attention he gave my work. His criticism was constructive (and copious) and significantly improved the manuscript. Jonathan GS Koppell has contributed in innumerable ways to this project, beginning in winter 1997 when he said to me, "You know, that could be a good dissertation topic." Then my graduate-school classmate and now my husband, Jonathan has since become the world's number-two expert on self-financed candidates in congressional elections from 1992 to 2000. I could not have done this without him.

All remaining errors or shortcomings are, of course, my own responsibility.

CHAPTER I

Introduction

MENTION THE 2000 ELECTION CYCLE and most people think of butterflies and chads. But before the photo finish in Bush versus Gore (and *Bush v. Gore*), a different election held political junkies across the nation transfixed. In an open-seat election for the U.S. Senate in New Jersey, former Goldman Sachs chairman Jon S. Corzine shattered the previous record for personal spending in a statewide election, self-financing more than $60 million en route to defeating first Jim Florio, the former New Jersey governor, then Bob Franks, a moderate Republican congressman.

Corzine's victory inflamed a public debate on the impact of self-financers on American politics that simmered throughout the 1990s, coming at times to a full boil in response to the visibility of candidates like Michael Huffington, Steve Forbes, and Al Checchi. (The new mayor of New York, Michael Bloomberg, self-financed more than these three gentlemen combined, but he was crowded out of the editorial pages by September 11 and its aftermath.) Editorial writers urged "[reclamation of] the political system from the clutches of wealthy candidates" (*New York Times* 1996, A20). Reform advocates heralded the advent of "plutocracy" (Buckley 2000). And candidates who had to fend off rich challengers warned of "a government of millionaires who in effect will buy seats" (Sher, LaPolt, and Woods 1996).

The critical tone of commentators has been mirrored in congressional debate over campaign finance reform. During hearings on the Federal Election Campaign Act of 1971 (FECA), Senator John Pastore (D-Rhode Island) warned that without limits on personal spending "only the wealthy or those who are able to obtain large contributions from limited sources will be able to seek elective office. Neither situation is desirable and both are inimicable [*sic*] to the American system" (U.S. Senate 1971, 152). His colleague, Senator Frank Ross (D–Utah), agreed. "I think nothing is more important than to make running for political office available to any citizen of this country and to do away with the advantage given those who have great wealth" (U.S. Senate 1971, 159). Sixteen years later, Senator Pete Domenici (R–New Mexico) introduced a measure to help self-financers' opponents stay competitive. "Unless we are careful, Mr. President," Domenici cautioned from the Senate floor, "the congressional marketplace will become a Gucci boutique. . . . in a democracy we must not allow individuals who control vast wealth to enter the election booth with a big, sometimes unassailable, advantage" (U.S. Senate 1987b, S2685). Senator Dennis DeConcini spoke in support of Domenici's proposal.

> We are making elective office only available to a certain class of citizen. If this standard were always the way our leaders were selected this country would have missed out on having the leaders like Abraham Lincoln and Harry Truman—leaders of modest beginnings and no wealth. If we continue on this path and do not reform the system we are indeed in danger of having Mark Twain's remark "the best Congress money can buy" become the truth. (U.S. Senate 1987a, S7651)

Members of Congress spoke out against self-financers during consideration of the Bipartisan Campaign Reform Act of 2002 (BCRA), which included a variant of Domenici's fourteen-year-old proposal, now dubbed the Millionaires' Amendment. The amendment raised limits on individual contributions and party expenditures for candidates who face off against the deep-pocketed. Although some observers believed the Millionaires' Amendment was a self-serving ploy by congressional incumbents to maintain their traditional advantages (e.g., Harshbarger 2001; U.S. Senate 2001d), Senator Mike DeWine (R–Ohio) articulated his concerns in terms of political principles: "In essence, this struggle between rich and not so rich candidates really is a struggle for the soul of democracy" (U.S. Senate 2001c, S2539). On the House side of the Capitol, Representative Shelley Moore Capito (R–West Virginia) called the Millionaires' Amendment "a way to correct what I believe is one of the most glaring inequities in the current system" (U.S. House 2002a, H430). (Capito's view may have been influenced by experience—in 2000 her Democratic opponent self-financed $5.6 million in his primary and general election campaigns;

in the 2002 rematch she was anticipating when she uttered these words he ended up self-financing nearly $8 million.)

The plethora of public commentary on candidate self-financing stands in stark contrast to a dearth of theoretical and empirical inquiry. To date, political scientists have not provided a basic description of this controversial and increasingly prominent strategy in American electoral politics. Most scholarly references have been brief, with little or no interpretation. This book therefore fills a gaping hole in the political science literature, presenting the results of the first comprehensive investigation of self-financing in American congressional elections. It points not to a democratic system under attack from indiscriminate personal spending, but to a set of effects that require more subtle analysis and interpretation. Indeed, self-financed candidates have a spectacularly unimpressive batting average: the vast majority of candidates who rely on personal funds to pay for congressional campaigns strike out at the polls. Nonetheless, their participation in the electoral process has important consequences for democracy and representation. Focusing on self-financers also throws the political context into sharp relief, allowing refinement of existing notions of strategic decision making, the nature of political fund-raising, and the effect of campaign spending on election outcomes.

SELF-FINANCING AND DEMOCRATIC PRINCIPLES

In a game of Monopoly, each player starts with fifteen hundred dollars and the end result depends only on luck and skill. In an election campaign luck and skill are also important, as is the congruence between a candidate's political portfolio and the electorate's preferences. But money matters, too, and in the game of politics—unlike in Monopoly—players do not start off on equal footing. A candidate who is personally wealthy and willing to self-finance his political efforts seemingly enjoys a head start in campaign funding that gives him an automatic advantage over competitors with comparable political credentials. This advantage violates the principles of equal opportunity and fair play, deeply ingrained American political values.

The "loophole" in campaign finance law allowing candidates at any level of American public office to self-finance campaigns is a consequence of the Supreme Court's decision in *Buckley v. Valeo,* which overturned sections of the Federal Election Campaign Act of 1971. One FECA provision capped self-contributions at $25,000 for House candidates, $35,000 for Senate candidates, and $50,000 for presidential candidates, and FECA's defenders argued that these limits would reduce inequality among candidates. However, the Court found that "the ceiling on personal expenditures by candidates on their own behalf . . . imposes a substantial restraint on the ability of persons to engage in protected First Amendment expression" (424 U.S. 1, 12–59 (1976)).

Buckley may have settled the matter constitutionally, but in leaving personal spending unregulated it did nothing to assuage the concerns behind FECA's self-financing cap. Central to the legislative debate on FECA was the presumption that allowing unlimited self-financing in election campaigns undermines political equality. If personal wealth confers a political advantage, which is (and was) usually assumed, citizens who cannot bankroll their campaigns do not have an equal opportunity to promote their views or serve in representative government, regardless of their qualifications or political ideas. Of course, personal wealth is not the only potential source of political advantage. At any level of political office, candidates who already hold that office (i.e., incumbents seeking reelection) hold a significant edge over candidates who do not. It has also been established that candidates who have previously held *any* office, not just the one being sought, win much more often than candidates seeking their first elective position (Jacobson 1989; Jacobson and Kernell 1983). But the advantage of political experience does not offend our sense of fairness as much as the advantage of personal wealth does because it is earned in the political arena, not attained in the market sector or inherited, and is more relevant to a candidate's qualifications. Citizens do not have strictly equal opportunities to accrue political experience, either, since experience depends on past success, which in turn can depend on nonpolitical advantages. But past success also requires some political skill and hard work, and these are legitimate sources of political advantage.[1]

Political equality is important not only because it maintains fairness but also because it gives meaning to the electoral decision. As Stone et al. note, "The representative nature of the [American] system works best when two or more strong candidates compete for the support of their fellow citizens. . . . If citizens are to exercise the franchise in a meaningful way, the electorate must be offered a choice between or among candidates, and the flow of information to the electorate from the candidates or parties

---

1. The political advantage enjoyed by many relatives of prominent politicians is similarly unearned since it is not derived from political activity but from political inheritance.

competing for the office must be roughly balanced" (1998, 1). Senator Dick Durbin explicitly relates this problem to self-financing.

> People will show up with a lot of money in the bank, spend it on the campaign, and literally blow away any type of political opponent. Who loses in that process? The voters lose. If the system works as it is supposed to, you have a choice on election day. In order to have a choice, you have information about all candidates. That means you have an information source not only from a wealthy candidate but from someone who is not so wealthy. (U.S. Senate 2001e, S2540)

When one candidate enjoys a large advantage over the other(s), the absence of competition strips the vote choice of its meaning. In other words, a tremendous financial advantage can make an election so uncompetitive that it does not truly conduct citizens' preferences. Nor is it an exercise in accountability. This notion underlies complaints, frequently voiced by reform advocates, editorial writers, and self-financers' opponents, about self-financers "buying elections." The problem is compounded if wealthy candidates scare away potentially strong competitors, that is to say, if self-financing has a chilling effect on candidate emergence. Stone et al. argue, "Those concerned with the functioning of our democracy must be concerned if the strongest potential candidates do not put themselves forward for public office" (1998, 1), both because the electorate may have a shorter menu of choices and because campaigns may be less competitive.

The claims of reform advocates and editorial writers notwithstanding, self-financing does not universally undermine electoral competition. Indeed, it may actually enhance competition when self-financers challenge incumbents who might otherwise run without serious opposition. One political consultant has commented, "A challenger who cannot jump-start his own campaign might as well forget it" (Van Biema 1994, 35). Given a choice between weak opposition and solid, even if self-financed, opposition to an incumbent, surely small-*d* democrats should prefer the challenger who has enough funds to communicate with the voters and offer them a viable alternative.

Candidate self-financing has implications beyond electoral contests. One oft-repeated criticism of self-financing is that it undermines the representativeness of elected bodies by increasing the number of wealthy citizens serving in public office. After his 1994 battle against a candidate who self-financed $6.5 million, Tennessee's then governor Don Sundquist lamented, "People who founded this country intended for people to serve in public office from all walks of life, and . . . we're heading toward a government of millionaires who in effect will buy seats" (Sher, LaPolt, and Woods 1996, B1). Anticipating Jon Corzine's $35 million victory in New Jersey's 1998 Democratic primary for U.S. Senate, Sheila Krumholz of the Center for Public Integrity declared, "It's no longer a democracy but a plutocracy" (Buckley 2000). These comments imply that a government of millionaires is a bad thing, regardless of what the millionaires in government do, because it does not accurately reflect the distribution of millionaires in the population at large. As Norman Ornstein has argued, "Ideally, you want Congress to be a variegated group, people with diverse life experiences. You lose something if personal wealth becomes a criterion" (Van Biema 1994, 35).

Some self-financed candidates counter that financial independence allows them to pursue their constituents' interests without having to consider the wishes of campaign contributors. For example, U.S. Senate candidate Tom Bruggere (D-Oregon), who contributed nearly $1.5 million to his 1994 campaign, boasted, "No one owns me. I don't have special interests controlling me, and a $5,000 contribution won't buy me" (Walsh 1996, 26). This claim has also surfaced in campaign slogans: Herb Kohl, the Democratic senator from Wisconsin who owns a chain of grocery stores and the Milwaukee Bucks basketball team, campaigns as "Nobody's Senator but Yours," and the tagline of Jon Corzine's (D-New Jersey) television commercials during his 2000 campaign for U.S. Senate was "Unbought and Unbossed."[2]

WHAT DO WE KNOW ABOUT SELF-FINANCING?

The amount of energy, resources, and even hand-wringing devoted to the "rich candidate problem," as one editorial deemed it, should depend on the magnitude of the rich candidate's advantage. If self-financing has no impact on competition or election outcomes, then the normative concerns become moot. The *New York Times* has editorialized, "Congress has no more urgent task than to clean up a campaign financing system that

---

2. These three examples are all Democratic candidates, but there have also been many Republican self-financers in recent years. For some reason the Republicans have not provided good sound bites on this theme.

gives undue advantage to rich candidates" (1996, A20). But if the "undue advantage" is small, Congress may in fact have many tasks more urgent than the rich-candidate problem.

There has been surprisingly little empirical work in this area to date, so it is difficult to judge how much attention personal financing warrants from policymakers and others. The few political science accounts in the literature have been descriptive and (with one exception) brief. Crotty reports the names and personal expenditures of several candidates for House, Senate, and governor in the 1970 elections (1977, 126–30) and concludes from the track record of these eighteen candidates, fifteen of whom were unsuccessful, that

> personal wealth, of course, does not assure success in winning elections. It does place one, however, in a position to run for public office and it certainly does not hurt the campaign effort. Wealth, or access to it, may well play a far bigger part in defining the pool of eligible candidates for political office than has generally been realized. (1977, 128)

In his analysis of money in the 1974 and 1976 congressional elections, Jacobson (1980) notes that nonincumbents self-financed much more than did incumbents, and nonincumbents in competitive districts self-financed more, on average, than did nonincumbents in long-shot districts. Alexander echoes this finding: his tabulation of self-investments by House and Senate candidates in elections from 1974 through 1984 reveals that nonincumbents self-financed more frequently than incumbents (1986, 332). Herrnson identifies a similar pattern in the 1992 cycle (1995, 147, see table 6-3). In his study of congressional primary elections, Maisel finds that total spending is positively correlated with the amount self-financed but negatively correlated with the percentage of total receipts self-financed ([1982] 1986, 68–69). Jacobson (1997) reports candidates' preference of self-financing through loans, which can be repaid with raised contributions if the candidate wins, and self-financers' tendency to lose elections.

Clyde Wilcox (1988) has published the only article devoted exclusively to self-financers. His study of House and Senate candidates in 1983–84 presents summary data on self-financing by different types of candidates, including incumbents, challengers, winners, and losers. Wilcox finds that personal funds are an important campaign resource, especially when invested as "seed money," but concludes that "candidate investments do not seem to be having a major impact on electoral outcomes" (278). Wilcox uses such weak language for his conclusion because methodological limitations prevent him from specifying the marginal effect of self-financing more precisely (277). In a subsequent collaboration Wilcox revisits self-financing in a study of the timing of campaign receipts. Biersack, Herrnson, and Wilcox (1993) find that seed money, whether self-financed or raised, attracts later contributions, but campaign dough rises less if it is self-financed than if it is raised. The authors emphasize that

> self-financing may be a viable strategy early in a campaign for [inexperienced] candidates. Presumably, such a candidate needs to acquire name recognition in the district rapidly in order to collect individual contributions and to do well enough in benchmark polls to convince institutional actors that the candidate can mount a viable campaign. Early money from whatever source can help the candidate acquire the visibility to meet these ends. (1993, 545)

In the most recent contribution to this literature, Milyo and Groseclose (1999) evaluate the effect of incumbent wealth on campaign receipts, expenditures, and challenger quality. They conclude that personal contributions and loans are neither a significant source of incumbent campaign funds nor a deterrent to strong challengers.

The Theory of Strategic Politicians

The most important political science antecedent to this study is the theory of strategic politicians, named by Gary Jacobson and Samuel Kernell ([1981] 1983) but first employed by Gordon Black (1972). To understand how self-financing impacts the electoral system it is important to recognize the electoral context as a system of strategic decision makers whose political actions are instrumental to some degree. Self-financing itself is the outcome of a strategic decision; other candidates' reactions to self-financing also reflect strategic decisions.

To explain political decisions, political scientists have borrowed the idea of a utility calculation from economists. *Utility* itself is essentially the value an individual places on some condition. In a political context it is important to note that *value* does not necessarily mean monetary value—we can think of the value of being a member of Congress or the value of spending hundreds of hours on the campaign trail without attaching a price tag to either condition. Some have likened utility to satisfaction to divorce it from a monetary measure. A utility calculation is a simplified model of an individual's consideration of the pros, the cons, and the likely consequences of a particular course of action, such as running for office or lending one's own campaign a million dollars.

The theory of strategic politicians assumes that candidates (and other political actors) are rational decision makers who seek to maximize their utility. Political scientists have typically used the strategic-politicians thesis to explain potential candidates' decisions to embark on a campaign (Banks and Kiewiet 1989; Black 1972; Canon 1993; Jacobson and Kernell 1983), as will be done in the coming pages, but this book also extends the theory to candidates' decisions to spend their own money.

A generic utility function takes the form:

$$U_X = P_X B - C_X,$$

where

X is a course of action that can be taken in pursuit of some goal
P_X is the probability that X will result in achieving the goal
B is the utility the actor attaches to achieving the goal
C_X is the net cost of taking action X, including the opportunity cost (or forgone utility) of actions not taken
U_X is the net expected utility of taking action X.

In other words, U_X is a summary measure of the costs and benefits of taking action X. If U_X is greater than zero, the individual does X.

In chapter 2 we will consider U_{SF}, a candidate's utility of self-financing SF dollars, and in chapter 3 we will consider U_O, a candidate's utility of running for office, and U_S, a political party's utility of spending S dollars in support of a candidate. With respect to U_{SF} and U_O we will assume that a candidate's goal is to win; however, there is much evidence to suggest that some candidates do *not* run to win. Rather, they run to promote a policy, to give their parties a line on the ballot, to advertise businesses, or to pursue other goals not instrumental to victory (Canon 1990; Herrnson 2000). This book only considers such candidates briefly. Since this is essentially a story about how self-financing affects competition and election outcomes, candidates who are long shots or sure things are not of great interest. This study seeks to exclude those elections whose eventual outcomes were anticipated long before election day and those candidates who had no meaningful impact on the vote tally.

DATA AND METHODS

The story of self-financers is told using a combination of statistics and anecdotes. The primary research method is statistical analysis of an original data set of candidates for the U.S. Congress (House and Senate) in the 1992, 1994, 1996, 1998, and 2000 elections. The statistical analysis focuses on House elections for two important reasons. First, the data are available. The Federal Election Commission (FEC) collects detailed information in the form of candidate disclosure reports (mandated by sections of the Federal Election Campaign Act that survived the *Buckley* ruling) and employs data entry clerks to keypunch almost every entry into databases. These databases are made available to the public in the form of spreadsheets downloadable from the FEC's Web site (www.fec.gov). No other campaign regulator at the state or local level provides this information in such a user-friendly format. Second, the quantity and variation in congressional elections data are sufficient to allow statistical analysis. It is the only level of government with a big enough N for quantitative methods, and with many political variables marking substantive differences between candidates and districts, multivariate quantitative analysis is necessary to answer certain questions definitively. Certain patterns are evident in Senate data as well, but one cannot be as confident that those patterns genuinely represent the theorized relationships rather than peculiarities of particular campaigns. There are also significant gaps in the Senate data (discussed later) that limit their usefulness. The FEC data are complemented by more than a hundred additional variables; a complete description of each of the variables used in the text is provided in appendix A.

Case Selection: Potentially Competitive Nonincumbents

This study makes two important distinctions, between incumbents and nonincumbents and between potentially competitive and uncompetitive candidates. Ultimately, the focus is on potentially competitive nonincumbents in regular primary and general elections.[3]

3. All special elections are excluded from consideration. So are elections in Louisiana, where there are no party nominations, and 14 elections in Texas that followed the

Incumbents

Incumbent members of Congress very rarely contribute personal funds to their reelection bids (Alexander 1986; Herrnson 1995; Jacobson 1980; Milyo and Groseclose 1999). In the five cycles studied, less than 2 percent of incumbents seeking reelection self-financed $50,000 or more over the two-year cycle compared to 31 percent of the selected open-seat candidates and challengers. Incumbents' combined self-contributions and net self-loans in each two-year cycle averaged $5,045, compared to $180,662 for potentially competitive nonincumbents.[4] Indeed, House incumbents averaged *negative* $5,911 in contributions and net loans. This seemingly bizarre figure indicates that repayment of self-loans (including loans made prior to the 1992 cycle) outpaced self-contributions and new self-loans.

Because of the very small amount of variation in self-financing by incumbents it is, as a practical matter, almost impossible to study self-financing by incumbents. Moreover, incumbent self-financing is not theoretically very interesting. From 1992 through 2000 congressional incumbents won 93 percent of their reelection bids: for members of Congress victory is the default outcome. It seems unlikely that incumbents' advantage, already quite significant, is materially enhanced by an activity that almost none of them actually pursue, and research by Milyo and Groseclose (1999) confirms this.

Uncompetitive Candidates

Following Canon (1990, 1993) and Herrnson (2000) this book makes two important distinctions among candidates. The first distinction is between active candidates, who reported at least $50,000 in total campaign

---

Louisiana format after redistricting in 1996. Party conventions that award a nomination are also excluded from analysis of primary elections.

4. Note that the average for nonincumbents drops to $155,132 if just one of the 2,475 candidates is excluded. Jon S. Corzine, the former investment banker who provided more than $60 million to his 2000 Senate campaign, distorts any statistic computed with his values included as an observation. Indeed, because Corzine self-financed more than all other 1999–2000 cycle House and Senate candidates *combined,* he will usually be omitted from statistical analysis. If not, the numbers would tell a story about Corzine at the expense of hundreds of other candidates.

receipts from any source, and inactive candidates. Candidates who did not make the effort to secure at least $50,000 are assumed not to be serious about contesting an election and are disregarded in most of this book. The second distinction relates to the competitiveness of candidates' electoral jurisdictions. Candidates in *potentially competitive* elections ran in districts where their party averaged at least 40 percent of the two-party vote in the 1988, 1992, and 1996 presidential vote tally, or, for Senate candidates, they ran in a state that had elected at least one copartisan in a Senate or gubernatorial election from 1992 through 2000. (This criterion only excludes Democratic Senate candidates from Idaho, Utah, and Wyoming.) All candidates who challenged an incumbent from the same party were automatically deemed uncompetitive in primary elections; the 24 in-party challengers who defeated an incumbent had their eligibility reinstated for the general election. (If an incumbent lost the primary his seat is treated as an open seat in the general election.) For open-seat candidates in general elections, the definition of *potentially competitive* is further restricted to exclude candidates in districts where their party's average presidential vote exceeded 60 percent (for House candidates) or states where the other party did not win a gubernatorial or presidential election during the period (for Senate candidates), since these candidates were virtually assured of winning the general election the moment they received their party's nomination. These criteria do a good job of excluding uncompetitive candidates without also dropping competitive candidates. Only 12 of 3,896 nonincumbents deemed uncompetitive won seats in Congress, and only 71 (less than 2 percent) came close enough—receiving 40 percent or more in a general election—to have played any role in holding opponents accountable. Only 4 of 111 should-be shoo-ins lost in open-seat contests. As a group the excluded candidates had virtually no impact on the process of selecting representatives.

OVERVIEW OF THE BOOK

The first step toward understanding the effect of self-financing on the democratic process and its outcomes is to describe the distribution of self-financing and self-financers across contexts and candidates. This description is offered in chapters 2 and 3. Chapter 2 demonstrates that self-financing is not entirely haphazard; rather, distinct patterns in the data confirm the theory of strategic self-financing. Indeed, self-financing covaries with other political variables, most notably the political experience of the self-financer and the stage of the campaign. These variables are important determinants of electoral success, so it is important, when estimating the effect of self-financing on election results, to hold these factors constant. Like a score in Olympic diving or gymnastics, which is adjusted to reflect the degree of difficulty of the feat attempted, the success of self-financers should be understood in the context of their races.

Chapter 3 turns the tables, describing the effect of self-financing on features of the electoral landscape, specifically the caliber of candidates who faced self-financers and the allocation of political party resources. Unlike open-seat status, elective experience, or the other variables analyzed in chapter 2, opposition quality can be influenced by self-financing or anticipation thereof. That is, the participation of a self-financed candidate—or even the threat of such participation—may shape the field of other contestants. The prospect of facing lavish self-financing is an incentive for a potential candidate to forgo a contest, while strong opposition provides an incentive for—and may even require—candidates to spend their own money on a campaign. In fact, the analysis confirms both of these hypotheses. A candidate's potential to self-finance *does* deter experienced candidates from entering races under certain conditions. For an experienced politician running for Congress, every dollar in threatened self-financing reduces the number of experienced opponents he is likely to face in the primary. In contrast, self-financing by inexperienced candidates is not discouraging to other potential candidates at all.

Despite the deterrent effect of self-financing, the net correlation between self-financing and opposition quality in primary elections is positive. That is to say, even though self-financers deter some experienced politicians from running, they still face more experienced opponents than non-self-financers. This is true, I argue, because self-financed candidates who *do* face experienced politicians must spend a great deal to overcome the greater strength of their opponents. One must therefore distinguish between a priori and ex post facto predictions. Before the campaign ensues, one finds that the threat of self-financing reduces the number of experienced opponents; after the candidates in a given contest are set, one finds that a candidate who faces more experienced opposition will self-finance more.

Chapter 3 also considers how self-financing affects strategic decision making by political party leaders. Parties are rational actors whose goals include maximizing the number of seats they hold in Congress (Kolodny 1998). To support that goal, party leaders must determine how best to allocate funds across their nominees. Self-financing enters their calculations in two ways, signaling candidate viability (or futility) and self-sufficiency. These cues exert contradictory and complex influences on party support. Mapping the amount of personal spending against the amount of party support each candidate receives suggests that both parties withhold financial support from extreme self-financers, who do not need the financial help and who are often weak candidates; however, Republicans tend to support candidates who self-finance moderately, who may boost their candidacies into competitive range, and who also have nonfinancial assets to recommend them.

The impact of self-financing on electoral competition and vote margins is addressed in chapter 4. First I examine the degree to which candidates are evenly matched on the campaign battlefield, demonstrating that self-financing does *not* always open up a wide financial gap between candidates. In fact, challengers' personal spending is much more likely to enhance financial competition than to undermine it. The more challengers self-financed, the closer they came to matching incumbents' financial resources. When there is no incumbent in a contest—in open-seat races and out-party nominations—the message is mixed. For some candidates, self-financing contributes to an imbalance of funding among competitors. In other cases, personal funds erase some or all of a financial disadvantage.

A financial advantage does not always indicate a political advantage, so the relationship between self-financing and vote margins is inspected closely. To isolate the causal effect of self-financing on vote results I carefully specify a multivariate model, select an appropriate estimation method, and explain why this more sophisticated—but also complicated—analytical tool is necessary. The results of this empirical analysis will likely surprise many, especially those who believe that money dictates election outcomes and that the burgeoning amount of personal funds in congressional elections spells danger for democracy. Yes, some self-financers swamp their opponents financially, but they do not always—or even usually—bury their opponents at the ballot box. Self-financing does give some candidates an edge, but its average effect is quite small. Campaign contributions appear to be a much more productive means of financing campaigns, and reasons for this are considered.

This book focuses on elections but does not overlook the fact that elections are primarily significant as instruments, not ends. Elections are important because they determine who serves in public office and, to some extent, how. Thus the empirical analysis concludes by discussing self-financing in the context of the "electoral connection," to use David Mayhew's term. Chapter 5 suggests that self-financed candidates make different kinds of representatives from candidates who rely primarily on contributions to fund their campaigns. Self-financers are descriptively distinct from their colleagues; as one would expect, self-financers are significantly wealthier than other members of Congress. They are also less likely to engage in what Richard Fenno calls "two-way" campaigning, or interaction between the candidate and constituency, which thus entails some degree of learning and responsiveness on the candidate's part. A candidate engaged solely in one-way communication, essentially advertising, only transmits; he does not receive information back from the constituency.

These differences do not recommend self-financers as representatives. They are quite unlike the vast majority of citizens, even citizens in more affluent districts, and they are less likely than non-self-financers to confront and engage the citizens they seek to represent. Perhaps making up for these shortcomings, they may enjoy greater leeway than most of their colleagues in terms of their relations with and obligations to campaign contributors. Indeed, many self-financers explicitly make this argument in their campaigns. For example, U.S. Senator Mark Dayton (D-Minnesota) claimed during his 2000 campaign, "I won't be working for the wealthy or the powerful or the special interests. I don't need their money" (Hamburger 2000). However, once elected most self-financers assimilate very rapidly to the norms of fund-raising—only a small percentage continue to resist the charms of campaign contributors. This book only glances at the legislative behavior of victorious self-financers and finds that on one dimension, loyalty to one's political party, self-financers behave distinctively. Big spenders in the Republican Party are more likely than their copartisans to buck the party line, while Democratic self-financers tend to be slightly more loyal to the party. On the whole, though, there is no evidence of superior representation provided by wealthy self-financers.

Chapter 6 discusses the implications of the empirical findings of this book for political theory, politics, and public policy.

THE TRACK RECORD

This book begins with a puzzle: Why do self-financers lose so many elections? Table 1.1 groups potentially competitive nonincumbent candidates

TABLE 1.1.   Candidate Election Rates in Primary and General Elections,
by Chamber and Self-Financing Level: Active Nonincumbents in Potentially
Competitive States and Districts

	Primary		General	
	Winners (%)	N	Winners (%)	N
Senate				
Non-self-financer ($0)	70	90	46	63
Minimal self-financer ($1–$49,999)	46	118	11	54
Moderate self-financer ($50,000–BCRA threshold)	31	85	16	43
Extreme self-financer (above BCRA threshold)	42	31	40	20
House				
Non-self-financer ($0)	71	438	34	210
Minimal self-financer ($1–$49,999)	59	959	20	647
Moderate self-financer ($50,000–BCRA threshold)	43	277	21	208
Extreme self-financer (above BCRA threshold)	37	35	31	45

into four categories based on the amounts they self-financed.[5] The first
group is called *non-self-financers* and as one might guess includes only those
candidates who did not loan or contribute any money at all to their campaign committees. *Minimal self-financers* are candidates who *did* support
their own campaigns, but only modestly, with less than $50,000. The third
group, *moderate self-financers,* includes candidates who self-financed from
$50,000 up to the threshold amount established by the Millionaires'
Amendment to the Bipartisan Campaign Reform Act. For House candidates, the threshold is $350,000, and for Senate candidates the threshold
amount varies with state population.[6] Finally, *extreme self-financers* are
candidates who self-financed the threshold amount or more. Counter-
intuitively, candidate victory rates do *not* increase with self-financing. In
primary elections they even decrease quite clearly.

Does this mean that self-financing somehow causes candidates to *lose*
elections? This sounds a little crazy but is not impossible. In theory, vot-

---

5. The method for measuring the amount of self-financing from which these categories are constructed is discussed in the next chapter.

6. BCRA was enacted after the period covered by this study, so the Senate threshold
amounts are calculated as if BCRA had been in force. This means that the threshold
amounts vary across election cycles as well as states, depending on the state voting age population estimated by the Federal Election Commission for each election. See appendix A.

ers could find big spending so offensive that they punish self-financers by voting against them.[7] A more plausible explanation would be that self-financing is a tool that is used primarily by candidates who find themselves in difficult political situations. This possibility is addressed in the next chapter.

7. Several political consultants have personally told me that their polling turned up no evidence that voters either punish or reward self-financers for campaigning with personal money. The results of these polls are the proprietary information of the clients for whom they were conducted and thus cannot be officially cited or identified.

CHAPTER 2

The Distribution of Self-Financing

Candidate Quality, Timing, and the Local Context

In the weeks following the 2002 general election, a journalist was developing a report on the gubernatorial contests in Texas and New Hampshire. The common link between these two elections in very dissimilar states was that both had included a wealthy businessman among the major candidates. In Texas, Democrat Tony Sanchez, a banker, self-financed $60 million in his unsuccessful bid to oust incumbent Republican governor Rick Perry (Sanchez lost, 40 to 58 percent). In the New Hampshire election, an open-seat contest, Republican Craig Benson provided $11 million to his campaign and defeated Democratic state senator Mark Fernald, 59 to 38 percent.

The reporter wanted to explain why Benson had won and Sanchez had lost, and he wondered whether it had something to do with the style of campaign each man had run. As we will see in chapter 5, this idea has some merit. But in the case of Sanchez and Benson the answer was probably much simpler. As a Democrat in a state that had strongly favored Republicans in the preceding decade (no Democrat had won the governorship or a U.S. Senate seat in Texas since 1990), Sanchez had a very tough row to hoe, made even tougher by the fact that his opponent was an incumbent. In contrast, Benson was running on the banner that usually prevailed in New Hampshire. Benson was also running against a little-known state legislator, not a sitting governor.

Considered in isolation each of these two elections tells a different story about self-financing. An observer who looks only at the Texas campaign might easily conclude that self-financing is fruitless given the magnitude of Sanchez's personal spending and the meagerness of his vote tally. The opposite conclusion could be drawn from a cursory look at the New

Hampshire election: Benson self-financed $11 million, Benson won by a large margin, ergo self-financing bought the election. The truth about self-financing is somewhere in the middle. With neither political experience nor party label to help him, Tony Sanchez probably would have lost by an even wider margin had he not spent generously on his campaign. In contrast, Benson's personal spending almost certainly gets too much credit for his victory over Fernald.

These examples underscore the importance of considering self-financing in the context of the political environment of each race. To fully appreciate the role of self-financing in American elections, and to isolate the impact of self-financing from the impact of the political context on election outcomes, one needs to know whether self-financers tend to be more like Tony Sanchez or more like Craig Benson. For example, if candidates who self-finance heavily are usually found in open-seat contests one would expect them to win fairly often not because they self-finance but because it is much easier to win an open seat than to beat an incumbent.[1] If self-financers are usually political novices one should expect them to lose most of the time because they lack the honed political skills and existing support networks of candidates with experience in the political world. This chapter thus examines the distribution of self-financing in relation to other important political variables.

The patterns identified in this chapter also help us understand the relationship between personal spending and the balance of competition. Do self-financers overwhelm their opponents? The answer depends in part on what kinds of contests attract self-financing. If personal spending is focused on challenges to entrenched incumbents it might bring competition and accountability to elections that would otherwise be effectively uncontested. In other words, self-financing against incumbents has the potential to invigorate competition rather than to undermine it, as is commonly assumed. If self-financing is instead concentrated in open-seat races, it could strip the electoral system of its major source of competition. Before decrying the presumed unfairness of self-financing, as have so many

---

1. Among all major-party House and Senate nominees from 1992 through 2000, 51 percent of open-seat candidates (26 had no major-party opposition) and 7 percent of challengers were elected, suggesting that an open-seat nominee is about seven times as likely as a nominated challenger to win a seat in Congress. Challengers in potentially competitive elections fared slightly better, winning 11 percent of their contests.

critics, one should consider whether self-financing is used more often to help weaker candidates stay competitive with their opponents, or to help stronger candidates demolish their rivals.

To answer questions about what self-financers are like one must first specify what a *self-financer* is. This, in turn, requires a definition of self-financing. While self-financing can be conceptualized as a dollar amount or a proportion, here the focus is primarily on raw amounts, specifically a figure dubbed *maximum self-financing* by Clyde Wilcox (1988). Most self-financing takes the form of loans from personal funds or personally guaranteed by the candidate; because candidates sometimes repay self-loans during an election cycle the cumulative sum of candidate contributions and net loans at the end of a cycle can be a misleading statement of how much personal money was actually available to the campaign. *Maximum self-financing* essentially disregards the "never mind!" implicit in midcycle loan repayment. Cumulative contributions and net loans are tallied at the end of each Federal Election Commission reporting period; the maximum amount committed at any point during an election cycle is *maximum self-financing*. *Maximum self-financing* is tallied for three distinct periods: the primary election, the general election, and the entire two-year cycle.

To some political observers it may seem that the defining characteristic of a self-financer is total reliance on personal funds. That is, a candidate can self-finance without really being a self-financer as long as he or she also raises money from campaign contributors. Those who recall the fierce 1994 campaign for U.S. Senate in California would probably name Republican congressman Michael Huffington, not Democratic senator Dianne Feinstein, as the self-financer in that contest, even though Senator Feinstein loaned and contributed $2.5 million to her own reelection campaign. This distinction is worthwhile, so even though self-financing in this book means a dollar amount I will also refer to the percentage of total funds self-financed. The denominator of that percentage is maximum self-financing plus contributions received. However, the dollar amount is more meaningful as a measure of the potential advantage derived from self-financing. For example, one would not want to group Gary Kingsbury, a Democratic House challenger in 1994 who self-financed 100 percent of his $57,100 in campaign funds, with Phil Sudan, a Republican House challenger in 2000 who self-financed 96 percent of his $2.6 million in campaign funds.

As we explore the relationships between self-financing and political variables it will be useful to group candidates into the categories *non-self-financers, minimal self-financers, moderate self-financers,* and *extreme self-financers,* defined in chapter 1 (table 1.1).

THE DISTRIBUTION OF SELF-FINANCING: AN OVERVIEW

From 1992 through 2000 there were 2,339 candidates (all major-party nonincumbents) who qualified for this study by virtue of running in a regular House election in a competitive district or any Senate election in a competitive state. Unopposed candidates are disregarded for the time being, as are those candidates for whom maximum self-financing could not be separated into primaries and general elections, so this chapter considers 2,080 candidates altogether.[2]

The distribution of self-financing in primaries and general elections is summarized in table 2.1. The mean amount of primary-election self-financing (i.e., maximum self-financing through the preprimary reporting period) was $295,855 for Senate candidates and $50,709 for House candidates; the median amounts were $19,629 for Senate and $10,000 for House. To put these figure in some perspective, consider that the mean amount of primary-election contributions was $705,179 for Senate candidates and $114,630 for House candidates. The nonincumbents in this study self-financed about 29 percent of their total primary campaign funding.

In general elections, mean self-financing was $320,686 for Senate candidates and $39,762 for House candidates, while median self-financing was $0 and $1,713. Again, as a benchmark to judge these figures we can consider general-election contributions, which averaged $1.1 million for Senate candidates and $227,426 for House. Self-financing is apparently a less important funding source in general elections than primary elections, amounting to only about one-fifth of total funds.

---

2. Self-financing is not divisible into primary and general election tallies for 193 candidates in contested primaries. These candidates failed to report their financial activity to the FEC in the preprimary disclosure period, so their preprimary activity is subsumed in a quarterly report. It is thus impossible to determine which amounts should be credited to the respective primary and general elections.

Table 2.1 illustrates three notable aspects of the self-financing phenomenon. First, more Senate candidates self-finance, and Senate candidates self-finance more than House candidates. This will probably not come as a shock to many readers as it is well known that the scale of campaign budgets is generally larger in Senate campaigns, where candidates must appeal for votes statewide. Still, it is worth noting that the threshold for "extreme" self-financing is, in most cases, considerably higher for Senate candidates than for House contenders. In other words, extremeness is relative, and yet there are still more extreme self-financers in Senate elections than in House elections. This is what one should expect, given the differing rewards to self-financing in Senate and House elections. Candidates are more willing to risk personal funds on a campaign if the payoff is membership in "the world's most exclusive club."

Second, a majority of candidates self-finance sparingly, if at all.

TABLE 2.1. Distribution of Self-Financing in Primary and General Elections, by Chamber: Active Nonincumbents in Potentially Competitive States and Districts

		Senate	House
Primary elections			
Non-self-financer ($0)	Count	69	314
	Column %	25%	23%
Minimal self-financer ($1–$49,999)	Count	104	767
	Column %	37%	56%
Moderate self-financer ($50,000–BCRA threshold)	Count	78	244
	Column %	28%	18%
Extreme self-financer (above BCRA threshold)	Count	30	34
	Column %	11%	3%
Mean self-financing		$295,855	$50,709
Median self-financing		$ 19,629	$10,000
N		280	1,359
General elections			
Non-self-financer ($0)	Count	89	427
	Column %	57%	41%
Minimal self-financer ($1–$49,999)	Count	31	489
	Column %	20%	46%
Moderate self-financer ($50,000–BCRA threshold)	Count	23	115
	Column %	15%	11%
Extreme self-financer (above BCRA threshold)	Count	12	21
	Column %	8%	2%
Mean self-financing		$320,686	$39,762
Median self-financing		$ 0	$ 1,713
N		154	1,052

Note: Senate candidate Jon Corzine excluded from calculation of mean and median.

Third, self-financing is a more significant source of funds in primaries than in general elections. Primary candidates self-finance a larger proportion of funds than nominees, especially in House elections. This is likely because those candidates who make it to the general election are less prone to self-finance than those who lose. In other words, many self-financers are weeded out in the primary. Indeed, recall that the percentage of House candidates winning their parties' nominations decreases as self-financing level increases. There is a similar downward trend in winning percentage among Senate candidates, although extreme self-financers win almost as often as minimal self-financers in Senate races.

Among those candidates who do win a contested nomination, there is a close correlation between the amount self-financed in the primary and the amount self-financed in the general election (fig. 2.1). More than half of all candidates are in the same self-financing category in both stages of an election cycle. Notably, the correlation between primary self-financing and general self-financing is larger in incumbent challengers (Pearson's $r = .87$) than in open-seat races ($r = .77$). This is noteworthy because the strategic context of a challenge is quite different in the primary and general elections. In open-seat races candidates are likely to face similar opponents (high-quality nonincumbents) in both stages of the campaign, while a challenger faces very different opponents (low-quality nonincumbents in the primary and an incumbent in the general). That self-financing levels are so closely tied for challengers suggests that many challengers simply either are or are not prone to self-financing, regardless of the context.

Is self-financing primarily a substitute for or a supplement to fundraising? For some candidates self-financing is the principal (or only) source of campaign funding, whereas other candidates also raise ample sums from contributors. There is significant variation in fund-raising within each category of self-financing. Consider, for example, the contrast between two Republican House candidates who self-financed virtually identical amounts. In New Jersey's Seventh District, 2000 candidate Mike Ferguson raised $379,620 and self-financed $200,000 (35 percent of his total primary funding). Dane Watkins, who ran for Idaho's Second District in 2000, raised only $5,555 while self-financing $200,770 (97 percent) on his primary bid. Both candidates are denoted *moderate self-financers*, but intuitively we recognize that Watkins relied on personal funding more than Ferguson did. (Incidentally, Ferguson won his primary and Watkins lost his.)

Despite the within-group variation, it is clear that self-financing is generally used as a substitute for fund-raising. Candidates who self-finance

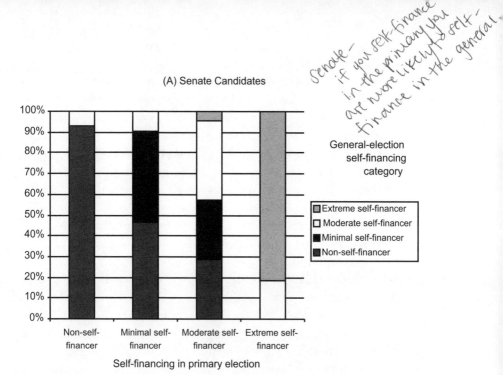

Senate –
if you self-finance
in the primary you
are more likely to self-
finance in the general.

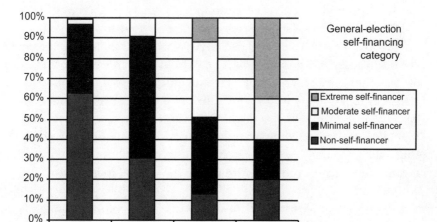

Fig. 2.1. Self-financing in general elections, by primary–election self-financing category and chamber

do not tend to raise much money, as is plainly revealed by the scatterplots in figures 2.2 and 2.3. Each scatterplot depicts contributions on the vertical axis and maximum self-financing on the horizontal axis, and each panel represents a different contribution source: individuals, political action committees (PACs), and political party committees. Figure 2.2 represents primary–election financing, and figure 2.3 depicts general–election funds. For any kind of contributions, candidates with high amounts of campaign contributions tended to self-finance very little, while candidates who self-financed generously tended to raise very little from contributors. Notably, the pattern is less pronounced for contributions from individuals than for contributions from PACs or parties. One might interpret this three ways. First, one might infer that institutional contributors, who have a finite supply of money and must prioritize how they allocate campaign contributions, choose to support the neediest candidates. In other words, contributors do not support self-financers because self-financers do not need support. However, there is ample evidence that candidate need is not the primary factor motivating campaign contributions, even to non-incumbents. Indeed, it seems clear that most institutional contributors support candidates whom they perceive as having at least a fair chance of winning (Sorauf 1992), in part because they want to be friendly with the winner who will be a new or continuing member of Congress. That outside financial support decreases with increased self-financing may be a signal that self-financers are perceived as weaker candidates unlikely eventually to be in a position to help contributors with legislation. Later in this chapter we will see more circumstantial evidence that this is the case. A third possibility is that self-financers do not receive contributions because they do not ask for them. One of the benefits a self-financing candidate enjoys is freedom from the phone. If one funds her own campaign, she need not devote several hours a day to "call time," when candidates are locked in a room with a phone and a list of individuals to call with pleas for support.

Self-financing does more than replace unraised contributions: self-financers tend to self-finance more than fund-raisers raise. Table 2.2 illustrates that candidates' total funding increases with their self-financing levels. This implies that self-financers' advantage consists not just of the freedom from fund-raising but also of an edge in overall funding levels. They do not have to spend their days trolling for campaign contributions, *and* they can afford more advertising, polling, and the like.

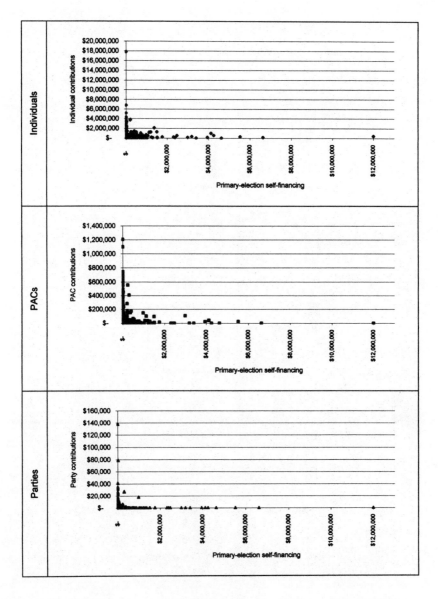

Fig. 2.2.   Self-financing and contributions in primary elections, by source of contribution (House and Senate candidates combined)

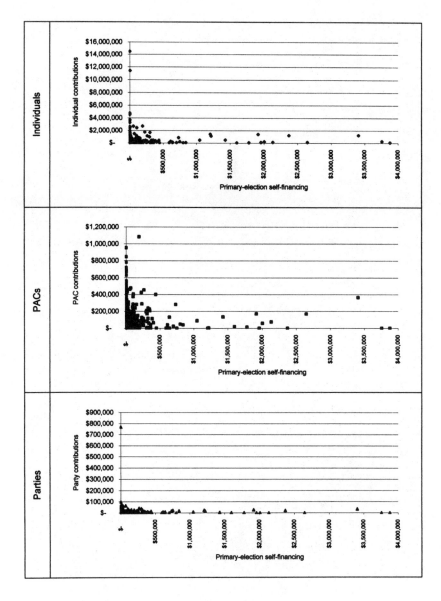

Fig. 2.3.   Self-financing and contributions in general elections, by source of contribution
(House and Senate candidates combined)

TABLE 2.2.   Average Total Funding in Primary and General Elections, by Chamber and Self-Financing Level: Active Nonincumbents in Potentially Competitive States and Districts

	Primary Elections		General Elections	
	Senate	House	Senate	House
Non-self-financer ($0)	$1,546,152	$ 169,515	$1,324,884	$ 268,803
N	73	316	92	398
Minimal self-financer ($1–$49,999)	$ 512,483	$ 112,951	$ 736,108	$ 206,443
N	108	770	33	457
Moderate self-financer ($50,000– BCRA threshold)	$ 625,225	$ 208,841	$1,492,772	$ 346,045
N	80	245	25	107
Extreme self-financer (above BCRA threshold)	$2,772,564	$1,038,012	$5,043,461	$1,317,746
N	29	34	12	22
All candidates	$1,029,792	$ 166,298	$1,658,168	$ 271,692
	290	1,365	162	984

Note: Senate candidate Jon Corzine excluded from calculations.

THE THEORY OF STRATEGIC SELF-FINANCING

Some variation in self-financing is surely idiosyncratic, and, as suggested earlier, some is due to individual candidates' fundamental propensity to spend or not to spend their own money in quests for public office. But some variation in self-financing is the consequence of rational calculations by individual candidates. A candidate must make a deliberate decision to write a check, cash in some stocks, or, as is often the case, guarantee a bank loan with the family residence. This decision may be a series of choices made as campaign expenses arise or it may be a general determination of projected funding sources made at the outset of a campaign. In either case, the candidate weighs the pros and cons of self-financing an amount SF, a process economists dub a "utility calculation." This calculation is represented by a simple utility function:

$$U_{SF} = P_{SF}B - C_{SF}.$$

U_{SF} is a candidate's net expected utility of self-financing SF, essentially the value (tangible or intangible) the candidate would get from self-financing SF, weighted by the probability of self-financing doing the trick and discounted by the costs of personal spending. If U_{SF} is greater than zero—that is, if the benefits exceed the costs—a candidate will provide *SF* to his campaign.

P_{SF} is the amount by which self-financing *SF* increases the candidate's probability of winning the election, *B* is the benefit he ascribes to winning the election, and C_{SF} is the net personal cost of self-financing *SF*. It is important to note that C_{SF} is not the dollar amount *SF* but the net utility of that amount if the candidate were to put it to his most preferred alternative use, which might be something entirely nonpolitical. As a candidate contemplates self-financing, say, $60,000, he might think about the relative satisfaction he would derive instead from buying a new BMW. If he opts for the ultimate driving machine he must raise money for his campaign from contributors; if he self-finances he does not have to bother with fund-raising. Thus the utility saved by *not* fund-raising is included in C_{SF}. In other words, if C_{FR} is the utility of resources—time, energy, and funds—that would be required to raise *SF* from contributors, and $C_{SF}^{\star}$ is the utility of the BMW (or whatever item the candidate will acquire with his *SF* dollars if he does not put them into the campaign), C_{SF} equals $C_{SF}^{\star}$ − C_{FR}. The costs of fund-raising include a candidate's time as well as the campaign resources that must be allocated to fund-raising such as consulting fees, postage, printing, or phone bills. These costs are not incurred if a candidate self-finances a given expenditure, so the utility of self-financing can be restated as:

$$U_{SF} = P_{SF}B - (C_{SF}^{\star} - C_{FR})$$
$$= P_{SF}B - C_{SF}^{\star} + C_{FR}.$$

The utility function suggests that certain conditions (associated with the elements P_{SF}, *B*, $C_{SF}^{\star}$, and C_{FR}) determine the level of self-financing. If these strategic conditions separately contribute to or detract from a candidate's likelihood of winning an election, one could easily confuse self-financing's effect on the election tally with the effect of the political context. The context also relates to the level of competition, which is meaningful for the functioning of democracy regardless of who wins or loses.

Strategic Conditions Represented in the Utility Function

A utility function is a somewhat abstract concept, but the elements P_{SF}, *B*, $C_{SF}^{\star}$, and C_{FR} are more than mere letters with subscripts. They are all symbols for very real features of a candidate's world. A prospective self-financer may not actually think, "Let's see . . . P_{SF} times B, minus C_{SF}^*, plus C_{FR} equals one hundred twenty-two point eight. That's more than zero—I'll do it!" But she probably does think about how many votes she is likely to gain by opening her own wallet, whether that number is enough to put her over the top on Election Day, and whether she would prefer to raise the money instead.

B is the value a candidate would derive from winning the election, that is to say, from holding office. The value attached to winning reflects the desirability of the office sought, which in turn depends on the nature of that office (would you rather be senator or dogcatcher?) and how badly an individual wants to win. The latter is a very subjective assessment for each candidate, but undoubtedly there is some relationship between wanting it and needing it. In other words, the utility of winning is related to a candidate's current position in the hierarchy of political office. The more vested she is in her political career, the more a candidate stands to lose personally if she loses an election. As Jacobson and Kernell note, "Running and losing, and in the process losing one's office base, not only interrupts a career, but may well end it" (1983, 22). In primary elections the winner only wins a nomination, not a seat, so the value of winning depends on how the eventual nominee is expected to fare in November— it is better to be nominated for a safe seat than to be a sacrificial lamb.

P_{SF} is the probability that self-financing SF will cause a candidate to win the election—how many votes he will convert and whether they will give him a victory. One way to think of P_{SF} is as the degree to which election results are sensitive to self-financing. Whenever or wherever campaign spending has a larger impact, P_{SF} is larger.

C_{SF}^* embodies the personal cost of self-financing. How much does a candidate want to spend his money on nonpolitical things? How much does she need to? Of course, what people *want* to do with their money is known only to them. But what they *need* to do with their money can be divined, at least roughly, from their personal wealth. Some people can afford to spend several thousand (or million) dollars on a run for Congress, but most do not have that luxury. Their personal funds must be directed to the mortgage payment or the utility bill or the kids' college tuition. Since candidate wealth is not a political variable (i.e., it has no direct bearing on election outcomes or competition), it will not be considered further in this chapter. However, it will prove convenient in later chapters to have identified a variable that affects self-financing levels but not election results.

TABLE 2.3.   Elements of the Self-Financing Utility Function

Element	Concept	Higher in / Increases with
P_{SF}	Probability of self-financing securing victory; campaign spending's effect on votes	Senate elections Primary elections
B (general elections)	Value of holding office	Senate elections Officeholding experience
B (primary elections)	Value of winning nomination	Senate elections Officeholding experience Favorable partisan contexts Open seats
$C_{SF}^{\star}$	Cost of self-financing	Wealth
C_{FR}	Cost of fund-raising	Favorable partisan contexts Open seats Officeholding experience

C_{FR} represents the ease or difficulty with which a candidate raises money. Some candidates have a knack for fund-raising, some have lists of previous contributors, and some just look like sure winners to PAC directors—these candidates can raise money relatively handily. Other candidates could spend the entire campaign soliciting contributions and still come up empty-handed. They may be asking the wrong people or making a ham-handed pitch, or they may be fundamentally unappealing as candidates. Whatever the source of a candidate's fund-raising ability (or disability), that ability affects the relative costs of fund-raising and self-financing as funding alternatives (table 2.3).

SELF-FINANCING AND THE POLITICAL CONTEXT

Let us now consider some concrete measures of the political variables represented in the utility function and explore whether real-life patterns match the predictions suggested by the theory of strategic self-financing.

Experience in Elective Office

Hubert Humphrey called fund-raising a "disgusting, degrading, and demeaning experience" (Adamany and Agree 1975, 8). He might have added that fund-raising is also demanding, as it requires a considerable investment of time and resources. The burden is heavier for some candidates than for others—fund-raising success depends on the skill, resources, and attractiveness of the candidate (Steen 1999). Candidates with previous experience in elective office tend to have more of all three qualities (Green and Krasno 1988), so they are likely to find fund-raising easier—and its appeal as a campaign funding option (relative to self-financing) greater—than candidates without elective experience, who struggle more to collect contributions. Because they are more skilled fund-raisers and also better bets in the eyes of rational contributors, one should expect to find experienced candidates self-financing less than inexperienced candidates. However, the strength of the relationship between self-financing and experience may be mitigated because experienced candidates have a strong incentive to self-finance once they have committed to a run. As noted previously, losing an election can represent a major personal and professional setback for someone who has made a career of holding public office. One should also expect to see experienced candidates self-financing more strategically than inexperienced candidates. Individuals who have successfully run for office in the past have likely developed the skills and knowledge to judge their political contexts more accurately than political amateurs can.

Indeed, there is a strong, negative relationship between political experience and self-financing, as is clearly apparent in table 2.4.[3] In both primaries and general elections for both House and Senate, as self-financing level increases the proportion of candidates with elective experience decreases markedly. In Senate primaries, the contrast is between non-self-financers and everyone else. Nearly 80 percent of all non-self-financers in contested primaries had held elective office prior to running for Senate, compared to just about one-third in each of the three other groups. House primaries tend to draw lower-quality candidates than Senate elections (Krasno 1994), but still 59 percent of non-self-financing House candidates had elective experience. Officeholding rates decreased with each category, to 42 percent of minimal self-financers, 33 percent of moderate self-financers and only 12 percent of extreme self-financers. A similar pattern is evident in general elections. Among Senate candidates in general elections, the drop-off in experience is still evident but slightly less pronounced than in primary elections. In House elections the proportions of experienced candidates in each self-financing category almost match the proportions in the corresponding primary category.

---

3. Whether the magnitude of correlation between self-financing and experience is attenuated by a countervailing incentive to preserve one's career cannot be determined.

TABLE 2.4. Proportion of Candidates with Experience in Elective Office in Primary and General Elections, by Chamber and Self-Financing Level: Active Nonincumbents in Potentially Competitive States and Districts

	Primary Elections (%)	General Elections (%)
Senate		
Non-self-financer ($0)	77	66
Minimal self-financer ($1–$49,999)	35	42
Moderate self-financer ($50,000–BCRA threshold)	33	43
Extreme self-financer (above BCRA threshold)	27	25
Total	44	55
House		
Non-self-financer ($0)	59	55
Minimal self-financer ($1–$49,999)	42	40
Moderate self-financer ($50,000–BCRA threshold)	33	37
Extreme self-financer (above BCRA threshold)	12	14
Total	44	45

The importance of this finding cannot be overstated. Political scientists have clearly demonstrated that experience in elective office is one of the best predictors (perhaps second only to open-seat status) of a congressional candidate's success (Jacobson 1989; Jacobson and Kernell 1983). Among the group studied here (potentially competitive nonincumbents in 1992 through 2000), 25 percent of experienced candidates won seats in Congress, and only 10 percent of inexperienced candidates did. Because self-financers are woefully deficient in this area their a priori chances of winning are quite low. When measuring the contribution of self-financing to candidates' success or failure rates, it is important to consider this baseline expectation.

The experience gap may also explain why outside financial support decreases with increased self-financing. Figure 2.1 showed that PACs and party committees give very little support to self-financed candidates; the people who hold the purse strings at these committees are professionals whose job it is to allocate their contributions wisely. They undoubtedly recognize the superior credentials of experienced candidates.

Timing of Self-Financing

"Early Money Is Like Yeast . . . it makes the dough rise." So advises the PAC EMILY's List, and their motto has been confirmed by political scientists. Biersack, Herrnson, and Wilcox describe three reasons why early funding is crucial to a campaign.

> First, an early campaign is needed to overcome the large advantage that most incumbents hold in name recognition (Mann and Wolfinger 1981). Second, early spending can facilitate fund raising by convincing important campaign-finance elites of the viability of the campaign.... Finally, PAC and party officials may look at early campaign receipts as one indicator of promising candidates. (1993, 536)

Testing the second of these three propositions, Biersack, Herrnson, and Wilcox find that funds collected early in a campaign tend to attract additional contributions down the road, and early fund-raising appears to raise more dough than early self-financing (Biersack, Herrnson, and Wilcox 1993; Wilcox 1988). Since early funding packs more of a punch than late money, strategic candidates should front-load self-financing. In other words, candidates who are willing to spend money on their own political campaigns ought to do so when they first jump into their contests. Thus, the time elapsed since a candidate's campaign debut is a good indicator of P_{SF}, the marginal effect of self-financing on candidates' chances of winning.

Despite the rewards to early funding there are also sound reasons to self-finance late. Many expenses—such as radio and television ads or direct mail—are incurred near Election Day. Candidates lose the earning power of their money or, as is frequently the case, pay interest on bank loans they have personally guaranteed, when they transfer personal funds before the campaign actually needs the money. In some sense, then, it is rational for candidates to self-finance late because late is when the bills are due.

To account for reasonable variation in self-financing due to the distribution of disbursements we will use a statistic called the *excess self-financing rate* to compare candidate self-financing to candidate expenditures in each of three time periods. For a single election (primary or general), the *early* campaign is the first FEC reporting period in which a candidate is active, and the *late* campaign is the last reporting period before the election. The *middle* period includes everything that is neither early nor late. The excess self-financing rate is calculated for each candidate and time period by subtracting the percentage of total election expenditures made during the period from the percentage of maximum self-financing committed during the period. To illustrate let us consider the primary campaign of

1998 U.S. Senate candidate Peter Fitzgerald, then a state senator from Illinois, who self-financed $5.5 million in his bid for the Republican nomination to challenge incumbent Democratic senator Carol Moseley Braun. During the first period in which he was an active candidate Fitzgerald reported very little financial activity of any kind, spending $44,151 (less than 1 percent of Fitzgerald's total primary expenditures of $5.3 million) and self-financing $26,986 (also less than 1 percent). Because the percentages are virtually indistinguishable, Fitzgerald's excess self-financing rate for the early period was +0 percent. From July 1 through December 31, 1997 (the middle period for Fitzgerald), he self-financed $2,875,000 (52 percent of his total) and spent $2,483,952 (47 percent of his total expenditures), resulting in excess self-financing of +5 percent. In the last reporting period before the primary, Fitzgerald self-financed $2,625,000 (48 percent) and spent $2,781,232 (53 percent). Fitzgerald self-financed a smaller percentage of his total than he spent in the late period, with extra self-financing of −5 percent. The *swing* in excess self-financing rate from the early period to the late period is an indicator of a candidate's "strategic-ness," or the degree to which a candidate front-loads his personal spending. Peter Fitzgerald's swing, from 0 percent to −5 percent, equals 5 percentage points. The larger the swing in excess self-financing, the more a candidate concentrated self-financing in the early stages of his campaign.

In primary elections the pattern of self-financing with respect to timing is quite clear: candidates obviously tend to front-load self-financing, committing larger percentages of personal funds (in comparison to expenditures) when the primary is more distant. Table 2.5 reports the average excess self-financing rate by period for primaries and general elections. The pattern is especially striking in House elections, where the excess self-financing rate decreased from +26 percent early in campaigns to −22 percent just before the primary, a swing of 48 percentage points. In Senate elections excess self-financing decreased from +14 percent to −11 percent, a swing of 25 points. In general elections self-financing also tended to come early, and the average swing was again larger for House candidates than Senate candidates. In House elections, excess self-financing swung 30 points, from an average of 18 percent in the early period to −12 percent in the late period. In Senate campaigns the swing was 17 points, from 10 percent to −7 percent.

Experienced candidates are more strategic actors, so do they behave more strategically when they self-finance? Yes, they do. The average swing

TABLE 2.5.   **Average Excess Self-Financing Rate in Primary and General Elections, by Campaign Period and Chamber: Active Nonincumbents in Potentially Competitive States and Districts**

Campaign Period	Senate		House	
	Mean (%)	N	Mean (%)	N
Primary elections				
Early	14	209	26	963
Middle	−3	281	−5	886
Late	−11	209	−22	964
Swing	*25*		*48*	
General elections				
Early	10	65	18	626
Middle	−5	43	−7	582
Late	−7	65	−12	626
Swing	*17*		*30*	

Note: There are fewer cases in the "middle" period because some candidates only filed two reports for a single election. Candidates who filed only one report in an election are excluded.

in excess self-financing from the early to late period was larger for experienced candidates than inexperienced candidates (table 2.6). In Senate primary campaigns the average swing was 22 percent for inexperienced candidates and 32 percent for experienced candidates; however, the difference is not statistically distinguishable from zero. Among House primary candidates the average swing was 44 percent for inexperienced candidates and 54 percent for experienced candidates, and the difference between the two House subgroups is statistically significant ($p < .05$ in a one-tailed difference-of-means test). In general election campaigns for Senate, inexperienced candidates had an average swing of 9 points, compared to 29 points for experienced candidates (the difference is not statistically significant). Among House candidates in a general election, the average swing was 28 points for inexperienced candidates and 32 points for experienced candidates.

Finally, let us consider whether the timing of personal spending relates to the raw amount self-financed. Did extreme self-financers spend their personal funds more or less strategically than other candidates? In table 2.7 the average swing in excess self-financing is listed for each category of self-financer separately, and one can plainly see the average swing decreased as self-financing level increased. In other words, extreme self-financers spent a much larger proportion of their personal funds toward the end of the campaign than did moderate self-financers, who spent a larger proportion in the late period than did minimal self-financers. The

TABLE 2.6. **Average Swing in Excess Self-Financing Rate in Primary and General Elections, by Candidate Experience and Chamber: Active Nonincumbents in Potentially Competitive States and Districts**

	Senate		House	
	Average Swing (%)	N	Average Swing (%)	N
Primary elections				
Inexperienced candidates	22	137	44	573
Experienced candidates	32	72	54	390
General elections				
Inexperienced candidates	9	39	28	383
Experienced candidates	29	26	32	243

decrease is in part attributable to the correlation between self-financing and experience—political veterans time their self-financing more strategically than inexperienced candidates, and the proportion of candidates with experience decreases as self-financing level increases. However, when experience is held constant the pattern is only muted and still persists. (To keep the table from becoming inscrutable experience is not included as a control.) Most notably, extreme self-financers in general elections do not tend to front-load personal spending at all. The surge in last-minute personal spending by extreme self-financers may be attributable to candidates who get close to the finish line and think, "Just another few thousand will put me over the top!" This sort of impulse self-financing may be evident only in extreme self-financers because minimal self-financers and moderate self-financers simply do not have the personal money to indulge the "Just another few thousand!" whim—they self-finance what they can afford early, then the personal wallet is closed.

This finding must be remembered when one evaluates the effect of self-financing on electoral success. Extreme self-financers' late expenditures look like last-minute decisions that are likely influenced by the anticipated outcome. No rational candidate with a commanding lead would dump personal funds into his campaign. When candidates self-finance because they think they might lose otherwise, it is tricky to determine whether personal funds actually improve their vote tallies.

Open Seats and Challenges

Like candidate experience, open-seat status is an important determinant of candidate success that correlates with self-financing, so one must take

TABLE 2.7.   Average Swing in Excess Self-Financing Rate in Primary and General Elections, by Self-financing Level and Chamber: Active Nonincumbents in Potentially Competitive States and Districts

	Senate		House	
	Average Swing (%)	N	Average Swing (%)	N
Primary elections				
Minimal self-financers	28	104	51	697
Moderate self-financers	26	77	42	228
Extreme self-financers	13	28	34	33
General elections				
Minimal self-financers	41	31	35	491
Moderate self-financers	−8	23	13	114
Extreme self-financers	0	11	−3	21

care not to confuse its effect on election outcomes with self-financing's. Open-seat candidates who win their party's nomination enjoy much better odds than nominated challengers, as half of them win and only 11 percent of challengers do. This makes seat status a good measure of the payoff to winning the nomination (B in the utility function for primaries). The contrast should be especially pronounced in House elections, where the gap between the success rates of open-seat candidates and challengers is wider.

In House primaries self-financing is indeed higher among open-seat candidates than among challengers. Figure 2.4 depicts the proportion of candidates seeking open seats in each of the four categories of self-financers with controls for chamber and prior experience. For both political veterans and those seeking their first elective office there is a clear albeit not dramatic pattern: the proportion of open-seat candidates steadily increases with self-financing level. Senate self-financing is not responsive to open-seat status.

A candidate who survives the primary in an open seat has a good chance of winning the election in November. This makes it easier for him to raise money from strategic campaign contributors, so in comparison to a challenger who may not be able to attract outside financial support an open-seat nominee should not need to self-finance as much. In other words, C_{FR} is lower for nominees in open-seat contests than in challenges, which in turn makes C_{SF} higher (because C_{SF} equals $C_{SF}^{\star}$ minus C_{FR}). This leads one to expect less general-election self-financing in open-seat races and more in challenges, but there is actually no clear relationship

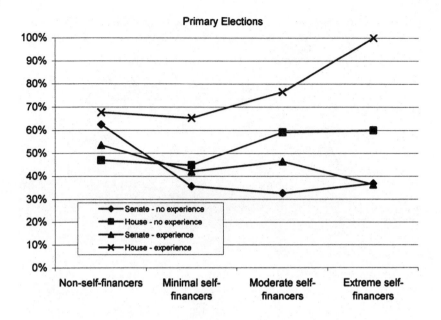

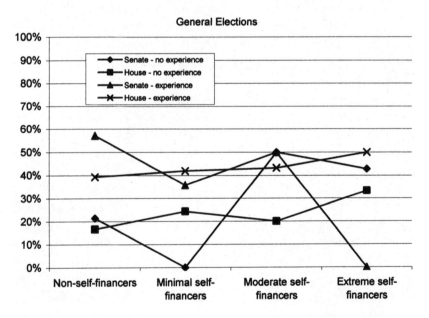

Fig. 2.4. Percentage of candidates in open-seat races, by self-financing level

between seat status and self-financing in general elections. As figure 2.4 illustrates, the proportion of open-seat candidates increases with self-financing but slightly in House elections; there is no pattern at all in the Senate races, with the proportion of open seats fluctuating up and down as self-financing level increases.

Normal Party Vote and Previous Nominee's Vote

Another important feature of each candidate's political context is the distribution of partisans in the candidate's state or district. This distribution obviously has a significant impact on the election results, as a district with more Democrats than Republicans is more likely to elect a Democratic candidate, and a district with more Republicans than Democrats is more likely to send a Republican to Congress, regardless of who self-financed and how much. A related but distinct concept is the distribution of support for a particular incumbent, deemed the "personal vote" by Cain, Ferejohn, and Fiorina (1987).

To measure each state or district's partisan makeup we will use the variable *normal party vote*. Based on the results of the most recent presidential election, the *normal party vote* is defined here as each candidate's party's share of the two-party vote, minus the national average. For example, if the Democratic presidential nominee received an average of 50 percent of the two-party vote nationally and 47 percent in a particular district, the normal party vote in that district would be −3 percent for Democrats and +3 percent for Republicans. We will also consider the previous nominee's vote, or the absolute percentage of the vote received by the district's previous nominee from a candidate's party, which is especially relevant in incumbent challenges as a measure of the degree to which the incumbent dominates.[4]

As measures of how a candidate's party has fared in recent elections in his congressional district, the normal party vote and previous nominee's margin are very good indicators of the payoff to winning the nomination (*B* in the utility function for primary-election self-financing). If the normal party vote in a particular district is 60 percent Republican, the

4. I describe the specific measurement strategies for these variables in detail in appendix A. Although *normal party vote* and *previous nominee's margin* are strongly correlated with one another ($r = .49$, $p < .001$), each variable independently explains considerable variation in candidates' margins.

Republican nominee stands a very good chance of winning the seat, Republican potential candidates are likely to jump into the race, and those who do run in the GOP primary have a strong incentive—the prospect of winning the nomination of the favored party—to self-finance. The Democratic contender in the same district is almost sure to lose the general election, so the nomination is worth less to candidates in the Democratic primary. For the Democrats in a Republican district, self-financing is a risky gambit with little chance of paying off in the long run, even if it helps secure the nomination. This dynamic is perhaps best illustrated by the 1998 election in the Eighth Congressional District of Massachusetts, a seat opened up by the retirement of Representative Joseph P. Kennedy II. This district would be a safe seat for any Democrat—in the 1996 election Bill Clinton ran 27 points above his national average here, and Joe Kennedy defeated the Republican challenger 84 percent to 19 percent. The 1998 Democratic primary attracted several local officeholders and two of the top three primary self-financers in all House elections from 1992 through 2000; the Republican primary attracted a sole contender whose campaign did not report a single dollar of financial activity.

Because candidates should self-finance more when the benefit of winning the nomination is higher, one expects to find a positive correlation between primary-election self-financing and the indicators *normal party vote* and *previous nominee's margin*. This correlation should be stronger where partisan cues have more influence on a candidate's prospects. For example, House candidates usually draw much less media attention than Senate candidates (Krasno 1994), which means that voters have less information on which to base their decisions and rely more on partisan cues. If candidates recognize that their electoral fortunes are more tied to the party in House races, self-financing should be more responsive to the normal party vote.

It is not as obvious how the normal party vote and previous nominee's vote should guide strategic self-financing in general elections. Their direct impact is possibly ∩-shaped, as candidates should self-finance most where self-financing is most likely to tip the scales in their favor, that is, in very competitive districts. Where one party (or incumbent) dominates, self-financing is unlikely to help a candidate from the dominant or the underdog party. However, this pattern might be obscured by the pressures of fund-raising. Candidates who are seen as likely winners (that is, those nominated in districts that have recently favored their party) can attract campaign contributions from access-seeking donors, while candidates who are seen as long shots have difficulty persuading contributors to invest in their candidacies. The likely losers therefore have more reason to self-finance than the likely winners.

Table 2.8 lists the correlation (Pearson's *r*) between self-financing and the two measures of party support. It reveals four noteworthy findings. First, partisan indicators only appear to influence House candidates. Neither the previous nominee's vote nor the normal party vote is significantly correlated with self-financing by Senate candidates in primaries or general elections. This is consistent with the idea that Senate elections focus more on the individual candidates than House elections. Second, partisan indicators only influence self-financing in primaries. This is also expected because the partisan context offers a strong incentive to self-finance in the primary but mixed incentives in the general.

Third, partisan indicators influence inexperienced candidates more than experienced candidates. The difference between experienced and inexperienced candidates contradicts the expectation that experienced politicians are more sensitive to contextual signals. However, it is consistent with the idea that partisan cues have a stronger influence on self-financing by those candidates whose prospects are determined largely by party label. Inexperienced candidates, lacking a record of public service and a base of existing supporters, may recognize that their own (political) fortunes are closely tied to their party's strength, whereas experienced candidates can draw on their records and existing supporters to run more individualized campaigns. In other words, because district partisanship matters more to inexperienced candidates, their self-financing decisions are more sensitive to it.

TABLE 2.8.   Correlation (Pearson's *r*) between Self-Financing and Measures of Partisanship, by Candidate Experience and Chamber: Active Nonincumbents in Potentially Competitive States and Districts

	Senate		House	
	No Elective Experience	Elective Experience	No Elective Experience	Elective Experience
Primary elections				
Previous nominee's vote	.013	.006	.250★★	.112★★
Normal party vote	−.070	−.089	.170★★	.010
General elections				
Previous nominee's vote	−.022	−.052	.012	−.027
Normal party vote	−.122	.014	.056	.044

★★ $p < .001$

TABLE 2.9.   Correlation (Pearson's r) between Self-Financing and Measures of Partisanship in House Primary Elections, by Experience and Seat Status: Active Nonincumbents in Potentially Competitive States and Districts

	No Elective Experience		Elective Experience	
	Challengers	Open Seats	Challengers	Open Seats
Normal party vote				
Pearson correlation	−.041	.238**	−.057	−.003
N	404	376	200	401
Previous nominee's vote				
Pearson correlation	.098*	.265**	.023	.096†
N	307	293	152	291

†$p < .05$ *$p < .01$ **$p < .001$

Finally, the previous nominee's vote has more influence on self-financing than the normal party vote. In House primaries, the correlation between self-financing and previous nominee's vote is larger than the correlation between self-financing and normal party vote. An obvious explanation would seem to be that the previous nominee's vote is more relevant to House challengers, who would face the same opponent as the previous nominee, than normal party vote. However, the pattern holds up even when seat status is held constant. As table 2.9 demonstrates, previous nominee's margin has a stronger influence on primary-election self-financing than normal party vote even in open-seat races, where the previous nominee faced a different opponent.

DISCUSSION

This chapter has presented evidence that self-financing is neither uniformly nor randomly distributed across candidates and contexts. Rather, personal spending covaries with several political conditions, especially in House primary elections. These relationships help locate the baseline against which self-financers' successes and failures should be judged, although they offer somewhat conflicting suggestions.

The two most important lessons of this chapter relate to the timing of self-financing and the quality of self-financers. Indeed, time is the only feature of the strategic environment that consistently affects self-financing by many kinds of candidates. Candidates generally appear to recognize the strategic value of self-financing early in their campaigns. In both primary and general elections, candidates who self-financed at least one dollar tended to scale back their personal financial commitments as Election Day approached. The one exception was the group "extreme self-financers in general elections," whose average excess self-financing rate was highest in the period immediately preceding the general election. This pattern strongly suggests that for the wealthiest candidates, self-financing in October is influenced by endgame developments. As Election Day approaches, candidates get more and better information about their own standing, and those who can afford to make a final self-financed push appear to do so.

There are two potentially important implications of these findings with respect to timing. First, self-financing in moderate amounts may in practice be more effective than spending the family fortune—not because less money is inherently better but because the kinds of candidates who self-finance smaller amounts tend to invest their personal funds more wisely. In theory, self-financing extreme amounts could be a very productive electoral strategy, but actual extreme self-financers tend not to exploit their monetary advantage until it is too late to have a significant impact. Second, because extreme self-financing is probably correlated with late-breaking news, one must be especially careful not to confuse the effect of self-financing on outcomes with the effect of last-minute developments that both spur additional late self-financing and influence the vote.

Self-financing is also quite strongly related to candidates' backgrounds. The more a candidate self-finances, the less likely she is to be in the middle of working her way up the political ladder. This is especially true among House candidates but also applies to Senate candidates. Self-financers' lack of officeholding experience has at least two implications. First, self-financers' unimpressive track record must be regarded as at least partially caused by the political deficiencies associated with novice candidates. Of course, a lack of funding is often cited as a major liability for inexperienced candidates, and that is not a problem for self-financers; however, previous studies have shown that when campaign spending is held constant political experience still has a significant impact on candidate success. Personal money simply cannot buy a base of committed supporters or the campaign skills that many politicians develop on the way up the ladder. Second, because many self-financers have not previously run successful campaigns it is entirely possible that they do not know how to put their self-financing to its best use. A state senator or mayor is much more likely to have learned how to judge the political environment, including the advice she receives from her political consultants, than someone who has not held office.

In House primary elections self-financing was related to other strategic indicators, open-seat status, the normal party vote, and the previous nominee's margin. That self-financing in general elections is untempered by these important contextual variables is understandable because of the conflicting incentives they signify. When the context favors a candidate it is easier for that candidate to forgo self-financing and instead raise money from strategic contributors; however, self-financing promises the best return on the dollar when victory is in reach. More surprising is the absence of a correlation between self-financing and partisanship, incumbent strength, and seat status in Senate primaries. It is possible that there are simply too few Senate candidates for statistical patterns to emerge clearly but it is likely that there is a different dynamic in campaigns for the upper body, in which the prize for winning is more valuable. The promise of joining the world's most exclusive club trumps strategic considerations suggested by the state political context.

The same favorable conditions that motivate strategic self-financing attract the traditional breed of "strategic politicians," candidates with experience in elective office, to particular election contests. They also affect the calculations of party officials who determine how to spend party resources. The next chapter considers the dynamics among these types of strategic actors.

CHAPTER 3

How Self-Financing Shapes
the Field of Competition

Californians are famously blasé about earthquakes, but when an airline tycoon
named Al Checchi announced two years ago that he would spend tens of
millions of dollars from his own fortune to run for governor as a Democrat in
1998, the shock waves he sent through the Golden State's political establishment
were keenly felt. The mere idea of competing against a man worth $750 million
persuaded at least two top-tier Democratic prospects—U.S. Sen. Dianne
Feinstein and former congressman Leon Panetta—to skip the race.
—*Newark Star-Ledger,* June 13, 1999

Representative Frank Pallone Jr. Monday ended his exploratory bid for the
Democratic nomination in next year's United States Senate race, saying he could
not overcome the huge financial advantage of Jon S. Corzine, a political
neophyte whose wealth has made him a formidable challenger.
—*New York Times,* June 29, 1999

[Michael] Huffington was the Houston millionaire who had moved to
California, announced his candidacy [and] scared off more credible candidates
in the [1994 Senate] primary with his wealth.
—Ed Rollins, *Back Rooms and Bare Knuckles*

W HEN A MULTIMILLIONAIRE is accused of "buying an election" the
implication is that he has bought vast quantities of the tangible goods and
services that are thought to attract votes, like television ads, campaign
workers, direct mail brochures, and political consulting. But it may also
be possible to "buy" an election by scaring off the competition. Are Checchi, Corzine, and Huffington anomalies, or are they extreme examples of
a general pattern? In the debate over BCRA's Millionaires' Amendment
provision Senator Susan Collins suggested the latter. "I give [Millionaires'

Amendment sponsor Pete Domenici] great credit for bringing up a real problem in our campaign finance system of very wealthy candidates being able to self-finance their races. That discourages a lot of otherwise very qualified people from even running for office in the first place" (U.S. Senate 2001b, S2469).

This chapter explores self-financing's role in a dynamic political environment, emphasizing personal spending as an influence on, not just a product of, the strategic decisions of other political actors. Specifically, this chapter considers how self-financing affects the decisions of other potential candidates to run for office and the decisions of political party leaders to allocate financial assistance. If Al Checchi's promise to spend tens of millions influenced the decision of Dianne Feinstein—a popular senator with tremendous fund-raising potential *and* the capacity to self-finance generously herself—it is reasonable to hypothesize that lesser threats—say, a House candidate's promise to spend $100,000—would influence the decisions of local elected officials contemplating a congressional campaign, especially if running for Congress would require any of them to surrender a lower office. As the first part of this chapter will illustrate, the prospect of facing a deep-pocketed self-financer does indeed deter experienced politicians from entering congressional campaigns; nevertheless, self-financers face stronger-than-average opposition despite the "deterrent effect" of their personal wealth. Paradoxically, *prospective* self-financing has a *negative* effect on opposition strength, yet because facing high-quality opponents forces some candidates to dip into personal funds, *actual* self-financing is *positively* correlated with opposition strength.

Self-financing has the potential to influence another strategic decision: the allocation of political party resources. The most suggestive case is the candidate recruitment effort by Democratic Senatorial Campaign Committee (DSCC) chairman Senator Bob Torricelli (D-New Jersey). Torricelli's class of 2000 included Mark Dayton (an heir to the Dayton Hudson department store fortune) in Minnesota, Maria Cantwell (an executive at Real Networks whose stock holdings were valued in the millions) in Washington state, and Jon Corzine (former chairman of the investment bank Goldman Sachs) in New Jersey. Torricelli claimed that the personal wealth of these candidates allowed the DSCC to direct more money to Democratic nominees in other races. As he told the *Wall Street Journal,* "We knew from the outset it would be critical to have several candidates that do not need a subsidy from the national party. . . . Without Jon Corzine and Maria Cantwell, there would be no [Debbie] Stabenow [in Michigan] or Bill Nelson [in Florida] or a Brian Schweitzer [in Montana]" (Hamburger 2000, A28). One of Torricelli's predecessors at the DSCC, Senator Bob Kerrey (D-Nebraska) openly pursued a similar strategy in 1995–96, actively recruiting wealthy candidates in seven states (for a discussion of Kerrey's recruitment efforts see Bloom 1998, 2–5).

The second part of this chapter considers whether self-financing by wealthy candidates indeed frees up political party resources such that a party can offer more help to its nonwealthy, non–self-financed nominees. The evidence suggests that it does indeed, although there is a notable difference between the spending patterns of the Democratic and Republican Party committees.

THE SIGNIFICANCE OF OPPOSITION QUALITY

The first class of strategic decision maker analyzed in this chapter consists of experienced politicians, individuals who have already held an elective office, who contemplate running for Congress. The variable *experienced opponents,* defined for each candidate as the number of opponents with experience in elective office, represents two distinct political science concepts that share the name *candidate quality.* The first concept is the nature of alternatives presented to voters, in which the word *quality* connotes "qualification." Stone and Maisel have found that candidates with elective experience receive high scores, relative to inexperienced candidates, when rated on their integrity, problem-solving ability, dedication to public service, grasp of the issues, and ability to work well with others (Stone 1999), traits that are relevant to a candidate's potential to be a good officeholder. *Experienced opponents* is thus a measure of the number of well-qualified candidates in some elections. We are primarily interested in this concept as a dependent variable that is affected by personal spending.

The number of experienced opponents is also a degree-of-difficulty measure similar to contextual variables like district partisanship or seat status. The more experienced opponents a candidate has, the harder it is for her to win. Here *quality* refers to campaign prowess. Characteristics like political credentials, campaign skills, charisma, and a base of past supporters are collectively labeled *candidate quality* by political scientists, who agree that this somewhat nebulous concept plays an important role in determining election outcomes. These attributes are so intangible that po-

TABLE 3.1.   Victory Rate in Contested Primary Elections, by Number of Experienced Opponents and Chamber: Active Nonincumbents in Potentially Competitive States and Districts

Number of Experienced Opponents		Senate	House
0	Victory rate	64%	70%
	N	138	738
1	Victory rate	31%	36%
	N	128	472
2	Victory rate	24%	24%
	N	67	223
3	Victory rate	8%	15%
	N	13	55
4	Victory rate	0%	15%
	N	2	13
5	Victory rate		11%
	N		9
6	Victory rate		0%
	N		3
All candidates	Victory rate	42%	49%
	N	348	1,513

litical scientists disagree vehemently on how to measure them, yet they agree strongly that whatever *candidate quality* is, candidates with experience in elective office have more of it.[1] This aspect of *experienced opponents* is relevant as an independent variable that influences self-financing levels.

It is not intuitively obvious that two experienced opponents are harder to beat than one or easier to beat than three. But as the number of experienced opponents increases so does the probability that at least one of them is a formidable contender. Election results confirm this: among potentially competitive candidates in contested primaries there is indeed a very strong negative relationship between winning a nomination and the number of experienced opponents. As indicated in table 3.1, House and Senate candidates with no experienced opposition won about two-thirds of their contested primaries, and the winning percentage in both chambers decreased as the number of experienced opponents increased.

1. Some authors have suggested more nuanced measures of the quality of individual candidates (Green and Krasno 1988; Squire 1989); however, these alternatives are not significantly better predictors of electoral success than a dichotomous measure of elective experience, nor are they easily combined into a measure of the cumulative strength of multiple candidates.

Opposition experience also matters in general elections. Of course, candidates whose opponents have the most relevant experience—having been previously elected to the very seat in question—did quite poorly, defeating only 11 percent of incumbents in elections in states and districts that were potentially competitive for both parties. Open-seat candidates, whose opponents are almost universally weaker than challengers', obviously did much better, winning 51 percent of their general election contests (26 had no major-party opposition). Among open-seat candidates whose opponents had no elective experience at all, 54 percent won the general election. Open-seat candidates whose opponents had some prior service in elective office won only 44 percent of the time. Because opposition quality is a significant determinant of candidate success, the influence on opposition emergence is an important indirect effect of self-financing on election outcomes.[2]

WHAT'S SO SCARY ABOUT SELF-FINANCING?

Writing that potential opponents were "scared off" by Michael Huffington's willingness to spend his personal fortune on a campaign for U.S. Senate, Huffington adviser Ed Rollins dressed an unglamorous social science theory in unusually colorful garb. As employed by political scientists, the theory of strategic politicians posits potential candidates as rational decision makers who carefully weigh the costs and benefits of running for office against the costs and benefits of staying put. The decision calculus is formally stated:

$$U_O = P_O B - C_O,$$

---

2. Inexperienced opponents will not be considered here for a number of reasons. First, their decisions are simply not as consequential. Undoubtedly, some potential candidates without elective experience prove to be excellent officeholders, but as a group experienced candidates tend to be better qualified to hold public office. Candidates with elective experience also tend to be stronger electorally. Thus when experienced politicians are driven out of a race the voters generally suffer more of a loss—both in terms of the choices available to them and of the level of competition among the candidates—than when inexperienced potential candidates are deterred. Second, it is more difficult to detect patterns of strategic decision making among inexperienced candidates because their lack of experience makes them (as a group) poorer judges of the political environment than experienced politicians.

where B equals the benefit derived from holding a particular office, P_O is the probability of winning that office, and C_O equals the cost (or risk) of seeking the office, including the opportunity costs of forgoing other activities. If a candidate calculates that the net expected utility of running (U_O) is greater than zero, she will throw her hat into the ring; if U_O is less than zero she will stay on the sidelines. In plain English, if running seems to entail a lot of sacrifice with little chance of reward, a strategic politician will sit out an election. Running is its own reward for some candidates (Canon 1990), but this analysis concerns those whose goal is to win.

There are two principal ways in which self-financing can affect the decision calculus of other potential candidates: by decreasing P_O and by increasing C_O. A contribution of personal funds makes a candidate appear more competitive than one who self-finances nothing, all else being equal.[3] This perceived funding advantage, whether $10,000 or $250,000, is magnified by the fact that it can be put to use early in a campaign (Biersack, Herrnson, and Wilcox 1993; Jacobson 1997). Since a self-financed candidate should be a tougher rival than one who does not self-finance, ceteris paribus, a strategic politician who expects self-financed opposition downgrades his assessed chance of winning (P_O). The drop in P_O results in a lower estimate of U_O. The strategic politician concludes that running for office is not the best use of his time, energy, and other resources given the lower chance of winning. Opposing self-financing may also force the strategic politician to raise more money to stay competitive, thereby increasing his cost of running (C_O). In some cases, personal spending by an opponent will increase the strategic politician's costs enough to push him out of a contest he would otherwise have entered.

In the case of the 1994 U.S. Senate election in California, a minimum of eight Republicans (including one sitting congressman, two former congressmen, and a former U.S. senator) determined that, for each of them, U_O was less than zero. Each of these eight potential candidates signaled their interest in running by forming a fund-raising committee that was subsequently abandoned; it is impossible to know how many other Republicans decided against running before it was necessary to register a fund-raising committee with the Federal Election Commission. In an

---

3. Whether self-financing *actually* makes candidates more competitive will be addressed directly in chapter 4; however, there is no doubt that increased funding is generally *perceived* as enhancing a campaign.

election cycle that proved to be disastrous for Democrats, Huffington was the only Republican officeholder to challenge Senator Dianne Feinstein. Given the sheer number of Republican officeholders in California—46 state legislators (most of whom faced leaving office two years later anyway, thanks to term limits) and 22 congressmen at the time—this seems remarkable.

One should not blithely infer that the eight candidates (plus others unknown to us) who did not challenge Huffington in the Republican primary were "scared off" by Huffington's wealth. It is possible that they were instead deterred by the thought of having to raise enough money to pay for television advertising in California's nine media markets, or by personal considerations, or by Senator Feinstein's 17-point margin two years earlier when she ousted an appointed incumbent. Still, it is reasonable to expect that the prospect of facing a self-financed opponent in the primary influences experienced politicians' calculations, even if it is not always the deciding factor.

House campaigns usually attract less media attention than Senate campaigns (Krasno 1994), so it is harder to identify potential House candidates deterred by another candidate's self-financing. One example is the 1998 election in Colorado's Second Congressional District, an open seat centered in Boulder that was potentially competitive for both parties (Todd 1997). One would have expected the Republican primary to attract several candidates given such favorable conditions, and a local news report in late 1997 mentioned seven potential Republican candidates, including three officeholders (Sanko and Brinkley 1997). Five of them did not make the race, leaving extreme self-financer Bob Greenlee, who self-financed more than $800,000 and narrowly lost the general election, to face only token opposition for the Republican nomination.

Is Personal Wealth Scarier than a War Chest?

One should note the parallel between a self-financer's personal wealth and an incumbent's war chest. Both represent reserves that can be tapped at will, perhaps even used to level an opponent with early attacks before he has a chance to establish a positive image. Studies of war chests have followed logic similar to that presented here; for example, Goidel and Gross note that "incumbent candidates *may drive up the perceived cost of winning elective office* by . . . maintaining a relatively large campaign war chest"

(1994, emphasis added). Notably, the most recent work in this area concludes that incumbent war chests do *not* have a significant deterrent effect (Goodliffe 2001). Nor does incumbent wealth (Milyo and Groseclose 1999)—an even closer analogue to the nonincumbent wealth studied here.

If war chests and incumbent wealth don't scare off competition, is it reasonable to expect nonincumbent wealth to? The answer is yes. Personal wealth, war chests, and incumbency are all sources of candidate strength, and the relationship between strength and deterrence entails diminishing marginal returns. In other words, once a candidate is so intimidating that he is viewed as being nearly certain to win an election, no amount of war chest or personal wealth would have a discernible marginal impact on other candidates' decisions. This is in part because campaign spending does not have much impact on incumbents' vote tallies. Gary Jacobson explains,

> Incumbents, exploiting the extensive communication resources available to every member of Congress, saturate their districts with information about themselves, their virtues and services, before the formal campaign begins. Further campaigning produces, at best, very modest additional gains in support. (1990, 334–35)

Incumbents are very formidable candidates regardless of other circumstances, and only a small fraction of them—about 7 percent in the House and 13 percent in the Senate—lost reelection bids in the 1992–2000 cycles. Incumbency itself deters most potential challengers (Stone et al. 1998); those who are not dissuaded by the title "Member of Congress" are so few that the maximum potential impact of a war chest, or of incumbent wealth, is radically limited and therefore difficult to detect. If David is willing to fight Goliath he will not be deterred if he learns that Goliath has a bigger sword. Nonincumbents—especially the kinds of nonincumbents who rely heavily on personal funds (chap. 2)—are considerably less formidable as opponents, so personal spending has much more room to influence decisions.

What Factors Make Self-Financing More Daunting?

This conception of candidate strength and deterrence suggests that the deterrent effect of self-financing varies with the status of the seat sought by the self-financer, as well as by his political background, although the strategic-politicians theory can support conflicting hypotheses.

Challenges versus Open Seats

One might expect the deterrent effect to be weaker in out-party primaries (i.e., where the nominee will face an incumbent in the general election) than in open-seat primaries. That is, challengers are undaunted not only by incumbent wealth and war chests but also by self-financing by their opponents for the out-party nomination. Most candidates who run against incumbents—or who seriously consider doing so—are resistant to the charms of strategic indicators. Their very presence in contests they are almost certain to lose signals challengers' imperturbability in the face of discouraging contexts. If a challenger is willing to run against an incumbent, it is unlikely he will be significantly deterred by the prospect of self-financed opposition. The chance of winning the election is so close to zero that the prospect of self-financed opposition simply cannot depress P_O much more.

However, there are also compelling reasons to think that self-financing is less, not more, discouraging in open seats than challenges. The opportunity to run for Congress without facing an incumbent comes around infrequently, and a state legislator who has bided her time waiting for the local congressman to retire is unlikely to give up her big chance just because (as the legislator might see it) some rich guy thinks he can buy his way to Washington.

Experienced Candidates versus Political Novices

For similar reasons, self-financing by an experienced candidate might not affect potential opponents as much as self-financing by an inexperienced candidate, all else being equal. Experienced candidates are inherently strong opponents. Krasno notes,

> Challengers who have established political credentials attract more media attention than other candidates do. They have a track record and a proven base of support, assets that help establish their viability and may draw the notice of reporters. In addition, these challengers may be more likely to have the skills—including the organizational

and fundraising ability—necessary to wage highly competitive campaigns. (1994, 79)

Therefore potential candidates who are not already deterred by an experienced candidate's advantage are unlikely to be swayed by the prospect of his self-financing. Self-financing can do much more to boost the prospects of inexperienced candidates, who often have little to recommend them to voters and campaign contributors.[4]

One can also construct a reasonable argument to support the opposite claim. Green and Krasno have noted that "challenger spending is more productive in the service of a high-quality challenger" (1988, 893–94). Experienced candidates can advertise their past accomplishments, which may make their advertising more compelling than inexperienced candidates'. Also, experienced candidates may know better than novices how to spend campaign funds effectively. In chapter 4 we look at whether self-financing is also more productive when the self-financer is high quality, but it would be reasonable for a candidate to worry more about James Humphreys, a state senator from West Virginia who self-financed $3 million en route to a Democratic House nomination in 2000, than, say, any of "Kerrey's Millionaires," the businessmen recruited by DSCC Chairman Senator Bob Kerrey (himself a one-time self-financer) in 1996, none of whom joined Mr. Kerrey in the Senate.

Primaries versus General Elections

Logic dictates that the deterrent effect should be more pronounced in the self-financer's own party primary than in the opposing party's. As a potential candidate contemplates running she is not entirely certain about who her in-party opponents will be or how much they will self-finance, but she can be much more confident assessing the primary competition than sizing up the opposing party's nominee (assuming she is an open-seat candidate—if she is a challenger, she knows with virtual certainty that her opponent will be the incumbent member of Congress). Forecasting the behavior of one's general election opponent is a tricky task when one does not even know who that opponent will be.

---

4. In fact, Biersack, Herrnson, and Wilcox (1993, 546) find that early self-financing is more helpful to the fund-raising efforts of inexperienced candidates than experienced candidates and offer an analogous explanation.

House Elections versus Senate Elections

While some candidates gamble on running against a self-financer because their odds of winning the seat will never be better (in open seats), others may do so because the potential payout is significant (in Senate elections). As has been suggested, a seat in the U.S. Senate is considered by most a bigger prize than a seat on the House side of the Capitol. Just as candidates are more willing to self-finance in pursuit of a Senate seat, they may also be more willing to oppose a self-financer.

OTHER FACTORS SHAPING THE RELATIONSHIP BETWEEN SELF-FINANCING AND OPPOSITION QUALITY

Figure 3.1 depicts a model of the relationship between self-financing, in-party opposition quality, and out-party opposition quality. The model is derived from the theory that candidates are rational actors who hesitate to squander personal resources, whether those resources are financial (personal wealth) or political (a lower office).

The deterrent effect is represented by the arrows from *primary-election self-financing* to *primary opposition quality* and from *general-election self-financing* to *general opposition quality,* both labeled with minus signs. (*General opposition quality* is admittedly something of a misnomer, as candidates who lose a primary face no general-election opposition, and candidates who win a primary face only one major-party opponent in the general election; as is indicated in figure 3.1 the variable refers to the number of experienced candidates in the other party.) Figure 3.1 does not distinguish between House and Senate candidates, challengers and open-seat candidates, or experienced and inexperienced candidates, but the magnitude of the deterrent effect may vary with chamber, seat status, and candidate elective experience as discussed earlier. There is also an element of reciprocal influence: high-quality opposition may drive up a candidate's self-financing since competing against strong opposition makes it harder to muster support from contributors. (Many strategic contributors prefer to support likely winners, and strong opposition typically reduces any given candidate's chance of winning; see table 3.1.)

As illustrated in figure 3.1, part of the relationship between self-financing and experienced opposition is driven by other variables in the strategic environment. Jacobson and Kernell (1983) first suggest that high-quality candidates respond strategically to political contexts (specifically,

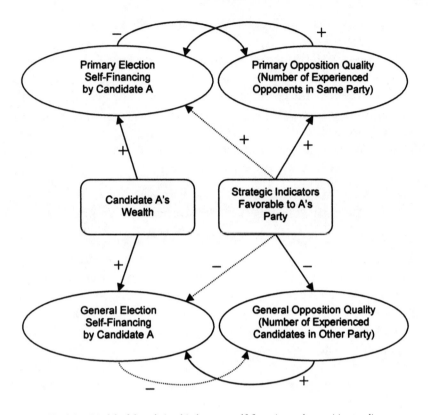

Fig. 3.1.   Model of the relationship between self-financing and opposition quality

presidential popularity and economic conditions) and tend to run when conditions favor their success. Subsequent tests of Jacobson and Kernell's theory of strategic politicians verify that candidates with experience in elective office respond to a variety of other external factors, including local partisan balance (Bianco 1984; Bond, Covington, and Fleisher 1985; Canon 1990), incumbent vulnerability (Bond, Covington, and Fleisher 1985; Krasno and Green 1988), past success by the candidate's party (Canon 1990; Jacobson 1990), and availability of an open seat (Jacobson 1990, 1997). This body of work suggests the plus sign attached to the arrow running from *strategic indicators* to *primary opposition quality*. Whenever the political context favors a candidate's party, he should expect vigorous competition for the party nomination.

Chapter 2 established that candidates in House primaries tend to self-finance when their electoral prospects are brightest. This expectation is represented in figure 3.1 by the arrow pointing from *strategic indicators* to *primary-election self-financing* with a plus sign next to it. The arrow is broken to indicate that this link is weaker than the link between political conditions and opposition quality. One should therefore expect strategic indicators to attract both experienced candidates and self-financers to many of the same primary contests. Because both self-financing and primary opposition strength respond positively to favorable political climates the deterrent effect of self-financing may be somewhat masked.

Conditions that favor one party's candidates spell difficulty for the other's. For example, an open seat in a district that splits its presidential vote 60 percent for the Democrat and 40 percent for the Republican will attract more Democratic candidates than Republicans. This dynamic is represented by the minus sign next to the arrow from *strategic indicators* to *general opposition quality*. In chapter 2 we saw that general-election self-financing is largely unresponsive to strategic indicators, so there is a weak arrow from *strategic indicators* to *general-election self-financing* marked with a minus sign. The deterrent effect is expected to be weaker in general elections given the difficulty of forecasting who one's general election opponent will be and how much that opponent will self-finance several months down the road. The arrow from *general election self-financing* to *general opposition quality* is broken to reflect this dynamic.

OPPOSITION QUALITY AND SELF-FINANCING

The universe for this analysis is the 1,656 potentially competitive candidates in contested primaries for whom primary self-financing is measurable (as defined earlier, "potentially competitive" primary candidates are candidates who reported receipts from all sources of at least $50,000 and whose state or district was competitive for their party). Figure 3.2 depicts the average number of experienced opponents facing candidates in each of four categories of primary-election self-financing. The figure clearly shows that average opposition quality increases progressively with self-financing level in both House and Senate primaries. This may begin to explain self-financers' poor track record in primary elections: many lose because they face strong opponents.

Controlling for the Strategic Context

The strategic-politicians thesis suggests that favorable political conditions like an open seat or candidate characteristics like political experience or

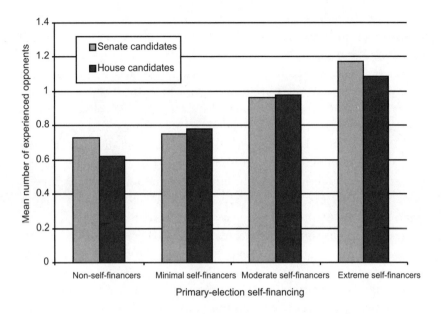

Fig. 3.2.   Average number of experienced opponents in primary elections, by self-financing level and chamber

incumbency magnify or diminish the deterrent effect. These political variables—as well as others—not only impact the magnitude of the deterrent effect, they independently influence a candidate's level of self-financing and the emergence of strong opponents. Statistical methods that hold such confounding variables constant are needed to reveal the relationship between self-financing and opposition strength.

To control for open-seat status and elective experience in House elections, candidates are divided into four groups: inexperienced challengers, experienced challengers, inexperienced open-seat candidates, and experienced open-seat candidates. In Senate elections, dividing candidates into four groups would leave fewer than 80 cases in three of the groups, rendering statistical analysis meaningless, so candidates are only divided into challengers and open-seat candidates. To control for other political variables multivariate regression is used.

The dependent variable, *experienced opponents,* is a discrete count variable ranging from 0 to 6 experienced opponents. The relationships among the variables are estimated using Poisson regression, a method particularly suited to "event count" variables for which events can be counted but nonevents cannot. Here we can count the number of experienced politicians running in a primary but we cannot count the number who decided not to run (see appendix B for a discussion of the relative merits of Poisson and least squares regression in this context). In a Poisson regression the effect of any one independent variable depends on the values of the other independent variables, so the regression coefficients are not interpretable in a straightforward fashion. Instead of reporting coefficients and then translating them into meaningful statements, I list the percentage by which the dependent variable changes (on average) with a one–unit increase in each independent variable. I call this transformation of a Poisson coefficient *percent change in prediction,* or PCP.[5] For example, if the PCP of an independent variable X equals .5, a one–unit increase in X increases the prediction of Y by 50 percent. It is important to note that an n-unit change in X changes the prediction of Y by $(1 + PCP)^n - 1$, not by $nPCP$.

Before forging ahead with multivariate analysis using a technique that will be new to many readers, let us consider as a baseline a Poisson regression with only one independent variable, primary-election self-financing. The PCPs for primary self-financing in each group are reported in table 3.2. For all six groups the PCP is positive, and in five of the six it is statistically significant. The positive PCPs show that when experience (for House candidates) and seat status are held constant, the number of experienced opponents for each candidate still tends to increases with primary self-financing. This illustrates why one must resist the temptation to point to a case like Darrell Issa, a 1998 Republican Senate candidate in California (who later won a House seat), and conclude, "Aha! That guy self-financed almost $12 million and still lost the primary—self-financing must not make a difference in election outcomes." Issa's loss probably had a lot more to do with his own lack of experience, which stood in marked contrast to the political résumés of his opponents, three-term congressman Frank Riggs and California treasurer Matt Fong (Fong was the primary victor). Like Issa, many self-financers lost their primary bids in large part because their opponents were experienced candidates with the political resources—name recognition, a knack for campaigning, an existing base of supporters, and the like—to neutralize the self-financer's monetary resources.

The PCP for Senate challengers is .010, which means that each $100,000 self-financed by a candidate in that group corresponds to a 1.0 percent

5. For those familiar with Poisson regression and its standard coefficient transformations, the PCP equals the incidence rate ratio minus one for each variable, or $e^{\beta} - 1$.

TABLE 3.2.   Poisson Regression: Number of Experienced Opponents in Contested Primary Elections, by Chamber, Seat Status, and Experience: Active Nonincumbents in Potentially Competitive States and Districts

(handwritten margin note: The More you self-finance, the More competition you see; correlation not causation; so as X goes up yy goes up.)

	Senate		House			
			Challengers		Open Seats	
	Challengers	Open Seats	No Experience	Experience	No Experience	Experience
Primary self-financing	.010	.026	.054	.412	.046	.010
	(4.46)**	(2.98)**	(1.97)*	(2.69)**	(9.32)**	(0.70)
Number of observations	168	122	394	191	375	405

Note: z-statistics of Poisson coefficients in parentheses; cell entries are percentage change predicted ($e^{\beta} - 1$). Standard errors adjusted to reflect clustering of observations within unique primary elections.

† $p < .10$ * $p < .05$ ** $p < .01$ *** $p < .001$

average increase in the number of experienced opponents he faces, compared to a similarly situated candidate. The increase is substantively quite small although statistically significant. Note that $100,000 "corresponds to" a 1 percent increase but does not necessarily "cause" it. To reiterate an important point, it has not been established that self-financing somehow attracts strong opposition, just that self-financing and high-quality opposition tend to coincide. The positive PCP may instead signify that contextual factors encourage both self-financers and experienced politicians to run in certain districts or that facing experienced opponents causes a candidate to self-finance more heavily. It is still possible that Darrell Issa (or other self-financers) might have faced even stronger opposition if he had not been able to chip in $12 million in personal funds. Later in this chapter we will sort out the various components of the bivariate PCP— the effect of self-financing on opposition quality, the effect of opposition quality on self-financing, and the effects of other variables on both. For Senate open-seat candidates the PCP is .026, which means that $100,000 in self-financing corresponds to only a 2.6 percent increase in the number of experienced opponents.

In House elections the PCP is positive in all four groups but with notable variations in magnitude. Most striking is the large PCP for experienced challengers, indicating that each $100,000 of self-financing corresponds to an average increase in the number of experienced opponents of 41.2 percent. Why is there such a strong relationship between self-financing and opposition quality in this group? The answer reveals a subtle aspect of the dynamics of campaign financing. There is not an extreme self-financer in the bunch, whereas the other groups have several, so the

PCP for experienced House challengers refers narrowly to the relationship between opposition quality and primary self-financing *when primary self-financing is less than about $300,000.* If one calculates separate PCP's for each increment of $100,000 it becomes apparent that in House elections the PCP decreases as self-financing increases. In other words, variation in self-financing is more strongly related to opposition quality at lower levels of self-financing. The difference between, say, $500,000 and $600,000 is not as important as the difference between $0 and $100,000.

This points to one of the challenges of telling a story with statistics. Statistics deal in averages, smoothing out the variations within groups. This is how analysts spot trends and patterns in hundreds of cases that seem unique when observed at close range. In this case, each self-financer has a different effect on and reaction to the context of his campaign, and the estimated PCP indicates the *average* across all the self-financing in the entire group. On average, $100,000 self-financed by an experienced challenger corresponds to a 41 percent increase in the number of experienced opponents he faces, and the estimated PCP does not distinguish between the first $100,000 or the last $100,000. But because the relationship between self-financing and opposition quality entails diminishing marginal returns, the true PCP is larger for the first $100,000 self-financed than the next $100,000 and the $100,000 after that and so on. This means that in a group where candidates only self-financed less than $300,000 (like experienced challengers), the overall PCP would be larger than in a group where candidates self-financed, say, $1 million even if the underlying relationships were fundamentally equivalent. For the extreme self-financers the group PCP averages the very strong relationship between opposition quality and their first $100,000 with the much weaker relationship between opposition quality and their last $100,000.

To account for a diminishing relationship one can transform the variable self-financing using a logarithmic or Box-Cox function. To keep the analysis consistent across chapters I have chosen the following transformation (discussed in appendix E).

$$f(\textit{self-financing}) = \frac{\textit{self-financing}^{.50} - 1}{.50}.$$

Now let us introduce additional political variables into the analysis to see whether the net positive relationship between self-financing and opposition quality holds up when the strategic context is taken into account.

The control variables include the contextual variables considered in chapter 2, *normal party vote* and *previous nominee's vote,* as well as dummy variables for members of a retiring incumbent's party (for open seats) and challengers to freshman incumbents. The local context is also gauged by Charlie Cook's first rating of the district's competitiveness, as published in the *Cook Political Report.* Nine dummy variables, combinations of party and year, capture national influences benefiting one party over another in a particular election year. The party-year variables also pick up the effects of party recruiting efforts and the effects of certain variables that are missing in particular years, like *previous nominee's vote* (unavailable for most districts in 1992 because new district lines were in effect). Finally, the variable *pool of state legislators,* the number of state legislators from a candidate's party divided by the number of congressional districts in the state, is included to control for variations that are simply a function of the supply of experienced candidates. (Details about the measurement and coding of each variable are provided in appendix A.)

The results of multivariate Poisson regression are reported in table 3.3. In all six groups the PCP of *f(self-financing)* is positive, and in five it is statistically significant, signifying that high values of self-financing and opposition quality go together even when strategic conditions are held constant. This initially seems not to support the hypothesis of a deterrent effect, but the relationship between self-financing and opposition quality operates in two directions. The reciprocal effects have not yet been disentangled—the results in table 3.3 indicate the magnitude of the *net* relationship between self-financing and opposition quality, which combines the effect of opposition quality on self-financing with the effect of self-financing on opposition quality.

One consequence of this relationship may be that the rate of primary-election success decreases as self-financing increases—not because self-financing caused people to lose elections, but because candidates who self-financed also happened to face stronger primary opposition. How much stronger? Consider, for example, inexperienced House challengers. The PCP for *primary-election self-financing,* reported in row 1, column 3 of table 3.3, is .202 ($p < .01$), indicating that with each one–unit increase in transformed self-financing predicted *experienced opponents* increases by 20.2 percent. "One unit" does not correspond to an exact dollar amount due to the diminishing marginal relationship. What does "20.2 percent more experienced opponents" mean in substantive terms? The answer depends on two things: the baseline to which "20.2 percent more" is compared and the degree to which primary success depends on the number of experienced opponents. Consider a hypothetical candidate whose predicted number of experienced opponents exactly equals the mean value for her group, .34, and who self-finances the mean amount in her group, \$48,383. Now imagine another candidate who is identical to the first in all respects except self-financing. The second candidate self-finances \$142,943, which corresponds to a one-unit increase in the transformation of self-financing ($f(\$142,943) - f(\$48,383) = 1$), and is predicted to face .41 experienced opponents. Such a small difference between these two candidates would only be meaningful if opposition quality exerted a gigantic influence on their respective chances of winning the primary.

The net relationship between self-financing and opposition quality is illustrated in figure 3.3. The slope of each line reflects the magnitude of the PCP, and the intercept is the average opposition quality for each group. Among House challengers, self-financing in large amounts corresponds to a substantial increase in opposition quality; however, in the other groups self-financing as much as \$1 million corresponds to an average increase of only about half an experienced opponent. Still, such a difference can have a significant impact on candidates' electoral fortunes, as we will see in the next section.

DOES SELF-FINANCING INFLUENCE THE QUALITY OF OPPOSITION?

It is important to remember that the relationships unveiled in the preceding section represent the combined effect of self-financing on opposition quality and opposition quality on self-financing. The statistical analysis to this point has not supported the hypothesis that self-financing decreases the strength of a candidate's opposition by deterring some experienced officeholders from entering an election contest, but such a deterrent dynamic would have been obscured if some candidates increase their personal spending *because* they face high-quality opponents. Indeed, a candidate battling against a strong opponent should be more inclined to dip into personal funds than one enjoying a cakewalk against a weak opponent. In other words, candidates who threaten to self-finance—explicitly, by vowing to spend "whatever it takes," or implicitly, by not promising *not* to self-finance—face fewer experienced opponents than candidates who are not expected to use personal funds. However, some of the prospective self-financers still end up facing experienced opposition and thus have to

TABLE 3.3. Poisson Regression: Number of Experienced Opponents in Contested Primary Elections, by Chamber, Seat Status, and Experience

	Senate		House			
	Challengers	Open Seats	Challengers, No Experience	Challengers, Experience	Open Seats, No Experience	Open Seats, Experience
Self-financing (transformed)	.050	.051	.202	.555	.040	.020
	(2.71)★★	(2.88)★★	(3.11)★★	(2.94)★★	(1.66)†	(0.37)
Normal party vote	.069	.013	.038	.017	.053	.027
	(3.31)★★	(0.73)	(2.34)★	(0.69)	(5.91)★★	(3.30)★★
Previous nominee's vote	.001	−.010	.024	−.006	−.007	.023
	(0.11)	(0.71)	(0.88)	(0.26)	(0.67)	(1.93)†
Freshman opponent	.080		1.747	.365		
	(0.13)		(4.32)★★	(1.01)		
Green/Krasno score	−.006	−.099	.078	.073	−.042	−.012
	(0.16)	(3.37)★★	(0.75)	(0.41)	(0.89)	(0.18)
Democrat—1994	.152	2.815	−.859	3.643	−.359	−.432
	(0.14)	(0.95)	(1.27)	(0.71)	(0.62)	(0.77)
Democrat—1996	2.156	1.694	−.895	1.104	−.708	−.528
	(0.85)	(0.95)	(1.75)†	(0.37)	(1.75)†	(1.17)
Democrat—1998	.430	2.140				
	(0.38)	(1.13)				

	(1)	(2)	(3)	(4)	(5)	(6)
Democrat—2000	−.322	−.988			−.379	−.161
	(0.31)	(3.23)**			(1.76)†	(0.75)
Republican—1992	−.189	.210	−.586	.088	.130	−.286
	(0.40)	(0.38)	(2.29)*	(0.12)	(0.34)	(0.97)
Republican—1994	.349	−.697	12.814	−.632	.686	−.174
	(0.45)	(1.17)	(2.78)**	(1.09)	(1.29)	(0.97)
Republican—1996	−.176	−.076	21.082	−.505	−.207	−.491
	(0.20)	(0.14)	(4.00)**	(0.59)	(0.52)	(1.37)
Republican—1998	.221	−.440	2.382	−.511		
	(0.29)	(1.02)	(1.41)	(0.51)		
Republican—2000	1.438	12.495				
	(1.06)	(3.59)**				
Pool of legislators			.016	.008	.003	.004
			(3.94)**	(3.58)**	(1.35)	(1.06)
Cook's forecast			.327	−.262	.125	.130
			(1.68)†	(1.40)	(2.33)*	(1.86)†
Same party as retiring incumbent					.667	−.126
					(1.91)†	(0.42)
Observations	164	126	313	156	318	353

Note: z-statistics in parentheses; cell entries are percentage change predicted ($e^{\beta} - 1$). Standard errors adjusted to reflect clustering of observations within unique primary elections.

† $p < .10$ * $p < .05$ ** $p < .01$ *** $p < .001$

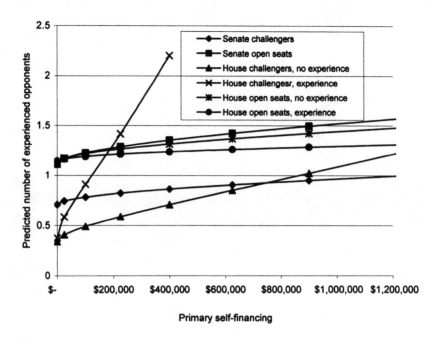

Fig. 3.3. Estimated marginal relationship between self-financing and opposition quality. (*Note:* *y*-intercept of each curve represents the mean number of experienced opponents within each group.)

make good on their promise to self-finance. The prospective self-financers who do not face experienced opposition do not actually have to use as much personal funding.

When two variables exert a simultaneous effect on one another, analysts typically use two-stage least squares (2SLS) regression to isolate the separate effects. However, the least squares model is not appropriate for this problem (see appendix B), and there is no Poisson analog to 2SLS. But framing the question in terms of *anticipated* self-financing instead of *actual* self-financing allows one to perform a two-staged process that will illuminate the deterrent effect. Framing the question in terms of the deterrent effect of anticipated or projected self-financing is not only methodologically necessary but conceptually appropriate. To claim that self-financing itself discourages experienced officeholders from running is not an accurate representation of the process. Experienced officeholders who contemplate running for office do not have crystal balls that show them exactly how much the other candidates will self-finance. Rather, they must base their decisions on whether or not to run on a projection (essentially a guess). The variable *anticipated primary-election self-financing* represents that guess.

The preceding section only considered candidates in *contested* primaries. If one wants to measure the impact of self-financing on election outcomes one should only consider races in which the outcome is not preordained. But now a different question is posed: who runs, not who wins. Some candidates may be unopposed *because* their potential to self-finance deterred others from running. The analysis is thus expanded to included all potentially competitive candidates, adding 344 candidates who were unopposed in primaries.

The Strategic Assessment:
Prospective Opponents Predict Self-Financing

How do strategic politicians size up the self-financing potential of a particular competitor? One can assume that experienced officeholders recognize the political incentives to self-financing that were discussed in the preceding chapter.[6] More important, they consider a rival's personal wealth as a significant determinant of his self-financing ability. If he enters the race very early (before July 1 of the off-year), when potential candidates have plenty of time to make up or change their minds about running, his early self-financing sends a powerful message to would-be opponents. And if he has run for Congress before, potential opponents will also consider how much he self-financed in the previous bid (or bids). The assessment of a particular candidate's projected personal spending can be represented by a linear equation:

$$
\begin{aligned}
\textit{Anticipated primary-election self-financing}_{Exp, Seat} \\
= \beta_0 + \beta_1 \textit{Candidate assets} + \beta_2 \textit{Candidate earned income} \\
+ \beta_3 \textit{Candidate unearned income} + \beta_4 \textit{Early self-financing} \\
+ \beta_5 \textit{Previous self-financing} + \beta_6 \textit{Normal party vote} \\
+ \beta_7 \textit{Previous nominee's margin} + \beta_8 \textit{Previous nominee's experience} \\
+ \beta_9 \textit{Previous nominee unopposed} + \beta_{10} \textit{Freshman incumbent} \\
+ \beta_{11} \textit{Retiring incumbent's party} + \beta_{12} \textit{Candidate quality index} \\
+ \beta_{13} \textit{Pool of legislators} + \beta_{14} \textit{Cook's early rating} + \beta_{15} \textit{Party} \times \textit{Year.}
\end{aligned}
\tag{3.1}
$$

6. Potential candidates who are not experienced officeholders may very well make similar projections; however, their lack of experience makes them poorer judges of the political environment, so deterrence of inexperienced candidates is difficult to discern. I have chosen to focus on experienced officeholders because they are more important for election outcomes and because they represent "high quality," meaning well-qualified, alternatives for the electorate.

The subscript *Exp, Seat* indicates that the equation parameters vary by candidate experience and seat status.

The indicators of candidates' personal wealth are coded from their Personal Financial Disclosures filed with the House Clerk and Secretary of the Senate. Unfortunately, the staff at the Secretary of the Senate's office were laudably diligent about destroying records one year after each election as prescribed by law.[7] Without this information it is impossible to create a reasonable post hoc "forecast" of what Senate candidates might have self-financed. One is thus unable to use statistics to learn whether the deterrent effect of Senate candidates Jon Corzine and Michael Huffington was typical, extraordinary, or somewhere in the middle. However, the results from House elections will be compared to anecdotal evidence from Senate elections.

The coefficients in equation 3.1 can be estimated with linear regression using *actual* self-financing as the dependent variable. Of course, strategic politicians do not sit at their computers running regressions and using the resulting coefficients to compute precise values of *anticipated primary self-financing* before they run for Congress. Nonetheless, estimates of *anticipated primary self-financing* generated by equation 3.1 are a reasonable proxy for the more impressionistic assessments made by strategic politicians. For the curious reader, full results for the first-stage regressions are reported in table 3.4.[8]

Once one has generated reasonable predictions of individual self-financing levels, one can use those predictions as an independent variable in a Poisson regression with *experienced opponents* as the dependent variable. The regression equation is the same as the one estimated in the previous section (table 3.3), except that *anticipated primary self-financing* is substituted for *primary-election self-financing*. While the coefficients of

7. Information from House candidates' Personal Financial Disclosure forms was collected in 1999, at which time the Legislative Resource Center of the House Clerk's office had disclosure forms dating back to 1992 available on their internal imaging system. Data for 2000 candidates was collected and data for Senate candidates was sought in February 2002.

8. To minimize the impact of extreme cases within any one of the four groups into which candidates have been divided, a single first-stage regression included all of the House candidates together. While this has the disadvantage of missing some patterns that are unique within a subgroup, its advantage is that it avoids overfitting the model. One should note that four cases with outlying values were omitted from the first stage, although values of anticipated self-financing were generated for those candidates based on the first-stage coefficients.

TABLE 3.4. First Stage Regression Results: f(anticipated primary self-financing): Active Nonincumbents in Potentially Competitive House Primary Elections

Earned income in previous year	0.08
	(3.64)**
Minimum value of candidate assets	0.00
	(1.82)
Minimum value of unearned income, previous year	0.09
	(6.16)**
Personal financial disclosure missing	1,263.38
	(0.07)
Early self-financing	2.07
	(16.23)**
Not a candidate before 7/1	17,126.70
	(1.54)
Self-financing in previous campaign	0.11
	(1.67)
Did not self-finance in previous campaign	1,265.82
	(0.09)
Open seat	4,452.23
	(0.47)
Elective experience	−4,761.27
	(0.25)
Normal party vote	922.58
	(1.75)
Previous nominee's vote	1,696.45
	(4.15)**
Freshman incumbent	−6,318.13
	(0.53)
Green/Krasno score	−6,361.13
	(1.31)
Democrat—1994	−71,324.26
	(1.71)
Democrat—1996	−70,947.55
	(1.73)
Democrat—1998	−10,925.51
	(0.24)
Democrat—2000	−63,218.91
	(1.47)
Republican—1992	2,057.02
	(0.13)
Republican—1994	2,980.71
	(0.14)
Republican—1996	−5,654.70
	(0.26)
Republican—1998	−23,647.51
	(0.98)
Republican—2000	4,644.58
	(0.19)
Constant	14,755.85
	(0.48)
Observations	1,693
R-squared	0.23

Note: t-statistics in parentheses. Standard errors adjusted to reflect clustering of observations within unique primary elections. Four outliers excluded from regression.

† $p < .10$ * $p < .05$ ** $p < .01$;   *** $p < .001$

primary-election self-financing represented an association without regard to influence, the coefficients of *anticipated primary self-financing* represent the effect of *anticipated primary self-financing* on *experienced opponents,* since the first-stage regression essentially purges the system of reciprocal influence.

Self-Financing and Candidate Deterrence

The results of Poisson regression with *anticipated primary self-financing* (transformed as described earlier) as an independent variable are reported in table 3.5, with the percent change in prediction for *anticipated primary self-financing* listed in the first row. The statistical results suggest three conclusions.

1. *Self-financing does deter some experienced candidates from entering primaries.* For open-seat candidates with and without elective experience, the PCP of *anticipated primary self-financing* is negative and statistically significant. The PCP is also negative, but not significant, for experienced challengers. This means that an open-seat candidate who can be expected to self-finance heavily—by virtue of his personal wealth and political conditions—faces fewer experienced opponents than a candidate who is not expected to self-finance much, all else being equal.

2. *The deterrent effect is stronger in open-seat races than in challenges.* Candidates who are undiscouraged by the long odds of defeating an incumbent in the general election are likewise undaunted by a self-financed opponent in the primary. In challenges, anticipated primary–election self-financing by inexperienced candidates certainly does not appear to dissuade experienced candidates from running, as in fact the average number of experienced opponents increases with self-financing. The PCP is negative for experienced challengers but not statistically significant. Potential open-seat candidates, in contrast, do appear to consider opposition self-financing as they decide whether to run, as the PCP for both inexperienced and experienced open-seat candidates is negative and statistically significant.

3. *Self-financing by experienced candidates is more dissuasive than self-financing by inexperienced candidates.* This conclusion must be drawn tentatively, as the statistical evidence is not strong. In open seats the PCP is −.252 for experienced candidates and −.130 for inexperienced candidates. In challenges the PCP is negative for experienced candidates and positive (but very small) for inexperienced candidates. (One should note that there is very little variance in opposition quality among experienced chal-

TABLE 3.5. Poisson Regression: Number of Experienced Opponents, by Seat Status and Candidate Experience: Active Nonincumbents in House Primary Elections

	Challengers, No Experience	Challengers, Experience	Open Seats, No Experience	Open Seats, Experience
Anticipated self-financing	.129	−.339	−.130	−.252
(transformed)	(0.76)	(0.68)	(1.85)★	(1.47)†
Normal party vote	.047	.025	.052	.032
	(2.83)★★	(1.07)	(6.27)★★	(4.18)★★
Previous nominee's vote	.063	.008	−.009	.018
	(3.13)★★	(0.37)	(0.96)	(1.84)
Freshman incumbent	1.669	.686		
	(4.48)★★	(1.73)		
Green/Krasno score	.013	.026	−.048	−.115
	(0.13)	(0.17)	(1.00)	(1.79)
Democrat—1994	−.999	7.542	−.181	−.275
	(4.18)★★	(1.11)	(0.29)	(0.42)
Democrat—1996	−.999	.299	−.575	−.362
	(4.50)★★	(0.11)	(1.24)	(0.67)
Democrat—1998	−.995	.941		
	(3.61)★★	(0.27)		
Democrat—2000	4,185.792	180,045.423	11,406,568.280	−.334
	(5.43)★★	(5.38)★★	(12.95)★★	(0.52)
Republican—1992	−.500	.032	−.328	−.175
	(1.86)	(0.04)	(1.53)	(0.77)
Republican—1994	10.361	−.695	.115	−.205
	(2.69)★★	(1.33)	(0.31)	(0.65)
Republican—1996	14.469	−.171	.584	−.148
	(2.97)★★	(0.16)	(1.19)	(0.42)
Republican—1998	2.081	−.506	−.069	−.349
	(1.22)	(0.54)	(0.17)	(0.85)
Republican—2000	.243	−.065	−.222	−.262
	(0.29)	(0.07)	(0.60)	(0.75)
Same party as retiring			1.100	.075
incumbent			(2.98)★★	(0.26)
Pool of legislators	.016	.014	.002	.006
	(3.06)★★	(3.49)★★	(0.74)	(1.59)
Cook's forecast	.277	−.233	.077	.105
	(1.29)	(1.45)	(1.48)	(1.59)
Observations	660	337	445	484

Note: *z*-statistics in parentheses; cell entries are percentage change predicted ($e^{\beta} - 1$). Standard errors adjusted to reflect clustering of observations within unique primary elections. Experienced open-seat candidates excludes one extreme outlier.

† $p < .10$ ★ $p < .05$ ★★ $p < .01$ ★★★ $p < .001$

lengers, which makes it difficult to detect statistically significant differences.) However, for neither pair is the difference between experienced and inexperienced statistically significant. It seems likely that self-financing by experienced candidates is more dissuasive—perhaps because experienced candidates can put self-financing to better use than inexperienced

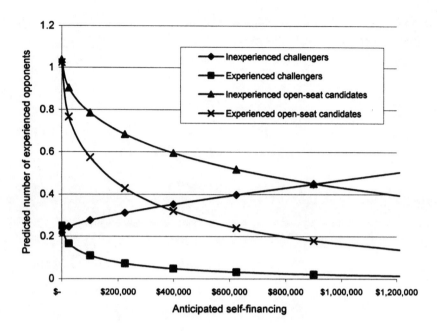

Fig. 3.4.   Effect of anticipated self-financing on predicted opposition quality (House candidates). (*Note:* y-intercept represents mean number of expereinced opponents within each group.)

candidates—but this may simply be an artifact of idiosyncrasies in the elections.

Because self-financing has been transformed to account for a diminishing marginal effect on opposition quality, interpreting the PCPs is complicated. Among inexperienced open-seat candidates the PCP for *anticipated primary self-financing-transformed* is −.13 ($p < .05$). When all other variables are held constant a one-unit increase in anticipated self-financing reduces a candidate's predicted opposition quality by 13 percent; however, the magnitude in dollars of "one unit" varies. It is thus easiest to convey the meaning of the statistics using pictures. Figure 3.4 illustrates the predicted change in opposition quality resulting from self-financing when the baseline is the mean number of experienced opponents to candidates in each group.

Figure 3.4 illustrates an important point with respect to challengers. As a group they faced very few experienced opponents, probably because many experienced politicians prefer staying in local office or a state legislature to taking the large risk of challenging an incumbent. Because so few experienced politicians even consider running in out-party primaries, there are not many opportunities for self-financing to deter anyone. This means that the deterrent effect would have to be quite strong to be detected. That we have failed to do so conclusively here is thus not surprising.[9]

HOW THE DETERRENT EFFECT HELPS SELF-FINANCERS

Consider hypothetical candidates A, B, and C who have no previous experience in elective office, are running for open seats, and are identical on every dimension except projected self-financing. Candidate A is not expected to self-finance at all, and by virtue of his other characteristics— which he shares with B and C—his predicted opposition quality is 2 experienced opponents. Candidate B is expected to self-finance $100,000 and is otherwise identical to candidate A, so her predicted opposition quality is 1.51. Candidate C is expected to self-finance $400,000 and is otherwise identical to A and B, so her predicted opposition quality is 1.35. The calculation of predicted opposition quality for B and C is shown in table 3.6.

By deterring experienced opponents, self-financers not only reduce the number of choices available to voters, they make their own campaigns easier from the get-go. Certainly it is better to face fewer experienced opponents, as table 3.1 clearly indicated that candidate success rates decrease as the number of experienced opponents increase. But we still do not know exactly how much candidates can improve their chances of winning through deterring opposition. How much better off is candidate C, with a prediction of 1.35 experienced opponents, than candidate A, with

---

9. A skeptic might still argue that I have not shown conclusive evidence of self-financing's chilling effect on candidate emergence. Perhaps what is really going on is that rich candidates tend to be strategic themselves and do not enter congressional primaries unless they are confident of facing weak opposition. Two pieces of information undermine this criticism. First, we have seen that many rich candidates actually *do* enter primaries against experienced opponents. Second, if one inspects the timing of candidate entry one sees that there is no relationship between entry timing and self-financing. On average, extreme self-financers in House elections enter a campaign about eleven days later than non-self-financers, seventeen days earlier than minimal self-financers, and sixteen days earlier than moderate self-financers. The differences among groups are not statistically significant. It thus appears unlikely that extreme self-financers wait to see the rest of the field before they declare their candidacies.

TABLE 3.6. Calculations of Predicted Opposition Quality Given Anticipated Self-Financing Open-Seat Candidates with no Elective Experience (PCP = −.130)

Candidate	A	B	C
Anticipated self-financing (÷ $100,000)	0	1	4
$f(SF) = \dfrac{\text{Anticipated self-financing}^{.50} - 1}{.50}$	−2	0	0.83
Marginal units of $f(SF)$, compared to Candidate A	0	2	2.83
Multiplier = $(1 + PCP)^{\text{Marginal units}}$	1	0.76	0.67
Predicted number of experienced opponents = Multiplier × 2	2	1.51	1.35

a prediction of 2 experienced opponents? One can translate the number of experienced opponents predicted into a probability of winning the primary using the rules of conditional probabilities and three simplifying assumptions.

1. A candidate's a priori chance of winning depends only on the number of experienced opponents.
2. The winning percentage of all candidates facing a given number of experienced opponents is a good estimate of any one candidate's a priori probability of winning. So, for example, since 59 percent of the inexperienced open-seat candidates who faced no experienced opponent won their nominating campaigns, one assumes that every inexperienced open-seat candidate who faced zero experienced primary opponents had a .59 a priori probability of winning.
3. The variable *experienced opponents* is distributed Poisson.

Let me elaborate on the third assumption briefly. For any given candidate the predicted number of experienced opponents is a function of a set of variables, the independent variables in equation 3.1. However, the observed number of experienced opponents is not likely exactly equal to the prediction. After all, actual opponents do not come in fractions. Rather, the observed number of experienced opponents is some non-negative integer, and the probability that it equals a *particular* integer, say, y, is given by the Poisson function, $(e^{-\lambda}\lambda^y)/y!$, where λ is the *predicted* number of experienced opponents and e is the root of the natural logarithum. Given these three assumptions one can approximate any candidate's a priori chance of winning given his predicted number of experienced opponents (λ) using the rules of conditional probability.

TABLE 3.7. Victory Rate in Primary Elections, by Number of Experienced Opponents and Candidate Experience: House Open-Seat Candidates

Number of Experienced Opponents	Open Seats, Inexperienced (%)	Open Seats, Experienced (%)
0	59	79
1	27	40
2	16	31
3	6	25
4	0	20
5	0	17
6	0	0

$$
\begin{aligned}
&\Pr(\text{Winning} \,|\, \lambda) \\
&= \sum_{j=1}^{n} \Pr(\text{Winning} \,|\, \textit{experienced opponents} = j) \\
&\quad \times \Pr(\textit{experienced opponents} = j \,|\, \lambda) \\
&= \Pr(\text{Winning} \,|\, \textit{experienced opponents} = 0) \\
&\quad \times \Pr(\textit{experienced opponents} = 0 \,|\, \lambda) \\
&\quad + \Pr(\text{Winning} \,|\, \textit{experienced opponents} = 1) \\
&\quad \times \Pr(\textit{experienced opponents} = 1 \,|\, \lambda) \\
&\quad + \Pr(\text{Winning} \,|\, \textit{experienced opponents} = 2) \\
&\quad \times \Pr(\textit{experienced opponents} = 2 \,|\, \lambda) \\
&\quad + \Pr(\text{Winning} \,|\, \textit{experienced opponents} = 3) \\
&\quad \times \Pr(\textit{experienced opponents} = 3 \,|\, \lambda) + \ldots \\
&\quad + \Pr(\text{Winning} \,|\, \textit{experienced opponents} = n) \\
&\quad \times \Pr(\textit{experienced opponents} = n \,|\, \lambda).
\end{aligned}
\tag{3.2}
$$

By assumption 2, $\Pr(\text{Winning} \,|\, \textit{experienced opponents} = j)$ is equal to the observed success rate for all potentially competitive candidates (in contested and uncontested primaries) who faced j experienced opponents. These success rates for open-seat candidates are reported in table 3.7. As the predicted value of *experienced opponents*, or λ, changes in response to *anticipated self-financing*, so does $\Pr(\textit{experienced opponents} = j \,|\, \lambda)$, and therefore so does $\Pr(\text{Winning} \,|\, \lambda)$.

Table 3.8 details the calculations for inexperienced open seat candidates with λ (predicted opposition quality) equal to 2. If candidate A's predicted number of experienced opponents is 2, he has a .14 chance of facing no experienced opponents, a .27 chance of facing one experienced opponent, a .27 chance of facing two experienced opponents, and so on. If he has no experienced opposition he has a .59 chance of winning the primary; if he has one experienced opponent his chance of winning is .27, and so

TABLE 3.8.   Calculation of a priori Probability of Winning a Primary Given
Predicted Number of Experienced Opponents (λ) = 2, Open-Seat Candidate with
No Elective Experience

j	Pr(NEO = j) = $e^{-\lambda}\lambda^j/j!$	Pr(Winning | NEO = j)	Pr(NEO = j) × Pr(Winning | NEO = j)
0	.14	.59	.08
1	.27	.27	.07
2	.27	.16	.04
3	.18	.06	.01
4	.09	.00	.00
5	.04	.00	.00
Total = Pr(Winning | λ = 2)			.21

Note: NEO = Number of Experienced Opponents. Entries in column 4 do not sum to .21 because of rounding.

on. Substituting these values into equation 3.2 reveals that candidate A is predicted to have a .21 chance of winning his primary. Repeating the process for candidates B and C estimates that their chances of winning their primaries are .27 and .29, respectively. In other words, self-financing $100,000 increases B's chance of winning from .21 to .27, while self-financing $400,000 increases C's chance of winning from .21 to .29.

Figure 3.5 illustrates the predicted change in chances of winning resulting from self-financing when the baseline is the mean number of experienced opponents to candidates in each group of open-seat candidates. Challengers are not depicted because the effect of challenger self-financing is not statistically distinguishable from zero. This figure essentially takes the predicted opposition quality depicted in figure 3.4 and converts it into a predicted chance of winning.

Because a diminishing marginal effect was assumed and operationalized with the transformation *f(self-financing)*, the biggest bang for the buck comes from the first $100,000 in anticipated self-financing, which increases candidates' a priori chances of winning by .05 for inexperienced candidates and .10 for experienced candidates. After the first $100,000 anticipated self-financing does not give much more help through discouraging potential opponents. Of course, actual self-financing may help candidates improve their chances once the campaign is under way.

Experienced Opponents in the Other Party

It was suggested earlier that strategic politicians in open seats would not be deterred by the prospect of self-financing in the general election be-

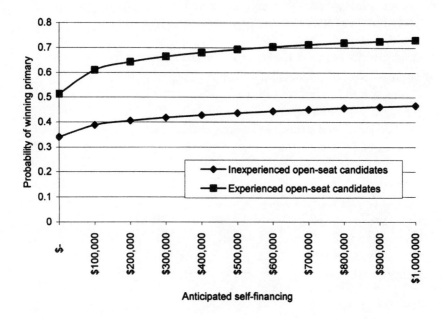

Fig. 3.5.   Estimated effect of anticipated self-financing on a priori chances of winning the primary. (*Note:* *y*-intercept represents baseline probability assuming the mean number of experienced opponents within each group.)

cause of candidates' uncertainty about their eventual opponents at the time of their decisions to enter a contest. This does indeed appear to be the case. Substituting general-election self-financing for primary-election self-financing and the number of experienced candidates in the other primary for the number of experienced candidates in one's own primary confirms my suspicion. For both inexperienced and experienced open-seat candidates, the amount of anticipated self-financing in the general election had no effect whatsoever on the quality of candidates running in the other party primary.[10] The Poisson coefficients were virtually indistinguishable from zero, substantively and statistically.

Recognizing that a candidate's anticipated self-financing in the general election would affect out-party politicians more if that candidate were expected to become the party nominee, I devised a weighting scheme for each observation. The weights were each candidate's likelihood of winning the primary, generated from a logistic regression of the variable *won*

10. Anticipated self-financing in the general election was generated using coefficients estimated for the open-seat *nominees* only.

nomination (one if a candidate won her primary, zero if not) on all of the available exogenous variables. So, for example, Joan Axinn, a Democratic candidate in New York's Fourth Congressional District in 1992, was predicted to self-finance $1,076,040 in the general election. However, Axinn was only predicted to have a 19 percent chance of winning the primary, so Republican candidates mulling the race would not likely have been deterred by the threat of facing her. (Having self-financed $338,000, Axinn was defeated in the primary by Phil Schiliro, a congressional aide.) In contrast Jane Harman was predicted to self-finance $859,708 in the general election for California's Thirty-sixth District in 1992 and was assigned a 76 percent chance of winning the primary. (Harman did win the Democratic nomination and went on to self-finance $700,000 in the general election.) Even with the weighting scheme, anticipated general-election self-financing had absolutely no effect on the number of experienced candidates running in the other party.

SELF-FINANCING AND POLITICAL PARTY SPENDING

Like potential candidates, party leaders are strategic actors whose behavior may be influenced by candidate self-financing. In this section we will focus on how self-financing affects the allocation of party spending. Our key assumption is that political parties have limited resources and prefer to spend money where it can have the greatest impact. The relevant utility function for party leaders is

$$U_{S,J} = P_{S,J}B - C_{S,J},$$

where S,J denotes spending S dollars to support candidate J, B equals the benefit derived from winning J's seat, P_S is the probability that the expenditure results in winning the seat, and $C_{S,J}$ equals the cost of the expenditure. As was the case in the self-financing utility function (U_{SF}), the cost of the expenditure is not the dollar amount S but the net utility of that amount if the party were to put it to the most effective alternative use, which might be spending S to support a different candidate.

The leaders who decide how to spend party funds might react to self-financing in two distinct ways. First, they might read self-financing as a sign of political viability. Viability entails many qualities that have little or nothing to do with personal wealth, such as personal appeal or political experience or ideological agreement with the constituency, but it is also true that a credible candidate is one who is likely to have sufficient funds to run competitively. Meeting that criterion, self-financers should be perceived as better investments than other candidates with similar political qualities and in similar political contexts.[11] In other words, $P_{S,J}$ increases with J's personal spending. One would thus expect to see parties investing funds in candidates whose personal funds make them competitive. In other words, self-financing may attract party support.

The strategy of 1999–2000 DSCC chairman Bob Torricelli suggests another possibility, of self-financing replacing party support. In other words, when a candidate is willing and able to adequately fund his campaign with personal money, his party need not use their precious resources to help him financially. $C_{S,J}$ may be high because the amount S would have more impact on another campaign. One thus expects extreme self-financers to enjoy less party support than other candidates.

Does self-financing by wealthy candidates indeed affect the distribution of political party resources across elections? This question is tricky to answer directly as one can only know how the political parties actually did allocate their contributions and expenditures given the slate of candidates who ran and the amounts each of them self-financed. One cannot know what the parties would have done under different circumstances.[12] Nonetheless, it is suggestive to consider the relationship between party support and self-financing among individual nominees. Did the amount spent by parties to help individual candidates depend on how much each candidate self-financed?

In chapter 2 we saw that self-financing by an individual candidate is negatively correlated with the amount of direct contributions that candidate receives from his or her political party (fig. 2.1). Parties can also support congressional candidates with *coordinated expenditures,* when party officials cooperate with the candidate's campaign staff to pay for certain activities (such as a public opinion poll or consulting fees), and, since 1996,

---

11. The caveat "with similar political qualities" is significant—recall that self-financers tend to be weaker candidates, winning much less frequently than non-self-financers (see table 1.1), in part because they often lack political experience (see table 2.4).

12. Analysis is complicated further by parties' increased reliance on soft money over the course of the 1990s, as there is no way to match soft money expenditures to individual candidates. Although soft money could not be used to fund "express advocacy," or explicit appeals to vote for or against congressional candidates, the parties were quite innovative in finding legally permissible ways to influence specific House and Senate elections without engaging in express advocacy.

independent expenditures, when the party directs and pays for activities that benefit a candidate without coordinating with that candidate or his agents in any way. The amount of coordinated expenditures allowed under the law is limited; the limits vary across states and election years and are based on each state's voting age population and a cost-of-living adjustment. For example, in the 1999–2000 election cycle the coordinated party expenditure limit was $33,780 in most House districts; the Senate limit ranged from $67,560 (in states with only one House district) to $1,636,438 (in California).[13] Independent expenditures are not limited.

The variable *party support* equals the sum of direct contributions, coordinated expenditures and independent expenditures. We begin with a simple comparison of mean party support across our four categories of self-financer, illustrated by figure 3.6.[14] Here the categories are determined by the tally of *maximum self-financing* across a two-year cycle (without distinguishing between primary and general election financing). Non-self-financers enjoyed the most party support in both House and Senate elections, but they were closely followed by extreme self-financers. It is thus not immediately apparent whether and how self-financing affected political parties' spending strategies.

As strategic actors who must determine how to allocate a finite number of dollars among candidates running on their tickets, the decision makers at national party headquarters are influenced by many of the same considerations that affect potential candidates' decisions to run for office and potential self-financers' decisions to commit personal funds to their campaigns. It is thus necessary to hold these factors constant using multivariate analysis to get a clear picture of the relationship between self-financing and party spending, with contextual effects pushed into the background. Table 3.9 presents regression results with the usual suspects held constant.[15] Separate equations are estimated for House Democrats,

13. The 2000 coordinated expenditure limit in states with a single House district was $67,560 for both House and Senate nominees.

14. A 1996 court decision allowed political parties to make unlimited independent expenditures on behalf of congressional candidates, so only candidates in 1996 and later elections benefited from party independent expenditures. However, the availability of this new tool did not appreciably increase total party support for potentially competitive non-incumbents, so segregating candidates into pre- and post-1996 elections does not further illuminate the basic relationship between party support and self-financing.

15. Limits on coordinated party expenditures, which vary by year and, in Senate elections, by state, are added to the regression as a control variable. The model assumes that

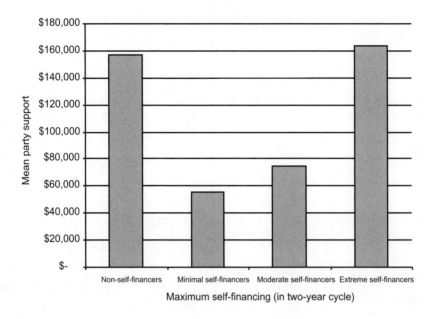

Fig. 3.6.   Mean party support, by level of maximum self-financing

House Republicans, Senate Democrats, and Senate Republicans, because party spending decisions for each of these four groups are largely made by distinct entities, the four congressional campaign committees (CCCs). The powers that be at the Democratic Congressional Campaign Committee, the organization with primary responsibility for supporting Democratic House candidates, may pursue a different resource-allocation strategy than the decision makers at the Democratic Senatorial Campaign Committee; the National Republican Senatorial Committee and National Republican Congressional Committee may well have different priorities than their Democratic counterparts.[16]

The regression model allows for the possibility that party spending may increase or decrease with self-financing, depending on a candidate's total level of self-financing. A preliminary equation included *squared self-*

---

variance in party spending depends on the coordinated expenditure limit and on the availability of independent expenditures as a tool for parties.

16. There may also be variation within party committees over time as there is a new chairman of each CCC every two years. We will not examine such variation here because the small number of candidates in a single election cycle, particularly in Senate races, renders single-election patterns undiscernible.

TABLE 3.9. Regression with Multiplicative Heteroskedasticity: Party Support for Potentially Competitive Nonincumbents in General Elections, by Party and Chamber

	House Democrats	House Republicans	Senate Democrats	Senate Republicans
Maximum self-financing (two-year cycle)	−591.50 (2.28)★			
Maximum self-financing, up to "turning point"		1,723.63 (0.85)	1,308.22 (0.23)	9,522.14 (2.40)★
Maximum self-financing, in excess of "turning point"		−1,295.63 (7.43)★★	−3,661.28 (3.40)★★	397.98 (0.09)
Limit on party coordinated expenditures	0.69 (1.72)†	0.99 (2.19)★	1.16 (9.56)★★	1.40 (7.51)★★
Open seat	8,587.50 (2.79)★★	8,036.02 (2.57)★	84,633.79 (2.86)★★	55,158.23 (1.45)
Elective experience	678.89 (0.16)	−7,869.58 (1.21)	−29,546.96 (0.53)	−67,062.68 (0.60)
Normal party vote	−156.97 (0.82)	247.81 (1.21)	1,008.81 (0.42)	4,468.95 (1.53)
Previous nominee's margin	291.42 (1.70)†	817.86 (3.80)★★	1,602.23 (1.45)	2,055.46 (1.68)†
Freshman opponent (challengers only)	4,755.47 (1.55)	8,297.82 (2.47)★	−80,001.56 (1.21)	−105,089.98 (2.19)★
Green/Krasno quality score	1,892.37 (1.81)†	3,920.84 (2.49)★	8,032.55 (0.74)	24,988.91 (1.17)
1994	8,451.71 (2.21)★	10,291.49 (2.37)★	−46,070.49 (0.67)	−111,506.27 (1.48)
1996	6,881.05 (2.09)★	−146.61 (0.03)	−46,683.78 (0.74)	17,698.86 (0.19)
1998	—a	—a	−29,882.76 (0.28)	−181,679.53 (1.94)†
2000	−2,740.05 (0.34)	−32,523.12 (2.75)★★	−153,758.76 (2.39)★	−220,754.70 (2.74)★★
Cook's forecast	−7,525.38 (5.71)★★	2,618.53 (1.39)		
Same party as retiring incumbent (open seats only)	−5,539.78 (1.11)	−9,409.88 (1.10)		
Constant	−4,686.76 (0.30)	−27,980.69 (1.52)	−23,285.53 (63.39)★★	−16,495.70 (0.52)
Observations	525	577	83	89
Turning point		$1,382,687	$1,774,196	$4,097,947

Note: z-statistics in parentheses. Standard errors adjusted to reflect clustering of observations among paired general election opponents. Variance of the disturbance is assumed to be a function of limits on party expenditures.
† $p < .10$ ★ $p < .05$ ★★ $p < .01$ ★★★ $p < .001$
a 1998 omitted due to multicollinearity

financing, and the estimated effects of self-financing on party support suggested by that preliminary equation are illustrated in figure 3.7. In this quadratic model the relationship between self-financing and party spending changes gradually (rather than dramatically shifting immediately at a

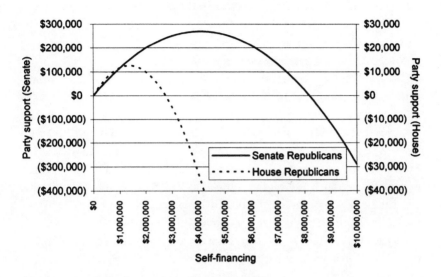

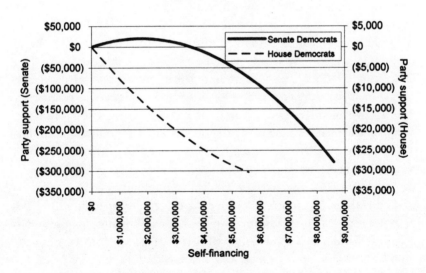

Fig. 3.7.   Estimated relationship between *maximum self-financing* and *party support*, by party and chamber

particular turning point); however, to avoid presenting an overly confusing set of regression coefficients I reestimated the model (for each party and chamber combination) assuming two constant effects, one below the turning point and one above the turning point. The turning point is set at the peak of each parabola depicted in figure 3.7.

Figure 3.7 suggests that the Democratic and Republican Party committees employ somewhat different strategies of funding allocation with respect to self-financing. The shape of the Republican curves (panel A) suggests that the Republican Party has been inclined to help those who help themselves, as party support initially increases with self-financing. However, that pattern reverses at a certain point ($1.4 million for House candidates and $4.1 million for Senate candidates), after which additional self-financing corresponds to decreased party support.[17] In contrast, the Democratic Party has been much less likely to support self-financers at any level. Among Democratic House candidates the relationship between self-financing and party support is consistently negative, with each $100,000 self-financed corresponding to a decrease of about $591 in combined party expenditures and contributions, on average. Among Democratic Senate candidates self-financing bears little relationship to party spending until candidates have self-financed about $1.8 million; after $1.8 million each additional $100,000 corresponds to an average decrease of about $3,700 in party support.[18] This seems to confirm that the Democrats were able to direct more resources to non–self-financers thanks to the financial independence of a few wealthy nominees, as claimed by DSCC chairmen Kerrey and Torricelli. In fact, the negative relationship between self-financing and party support among Democratic Senate nominees appears even stronger when 1998 candidate John Edwards (D–North Carolina), who is an outlier with $759,255 in party support and nearly $5 million in self-financing, is excluded from the mix.

While the regression results suggest specific party spending strategies responsive to self-financing, it is also possible that self-financing responds to party spending. Chapter 2 showed that extreme self-financers in gen-

17. It bears noting that only three Republican Senate candidates self-financed above the turning point, and the negative relationship between self-financing and party support is driven largely by one of them, Michael Huffington, who received less than $22,000 in party support for his 1994 Senate bid in California.

18. As usual, Jon Corzine is excluded from the analysis because his extreme self-financing, exceeding the combined total for *all* other candidates in 2000, overwhelms the statistics.

eral elections tend to spend most of their personal money quite late in the campaign. Perhaps very wealthy candidates self-finance as a last resort when they find themselves unable to attract financial support, including from their own party committees. So, as was the case with the number of experienced opponents, it is possible that the "effects" suggested by the regression coefficients of table 3.9 conflate the effect of self-financing on party support and the effect of party support on self-financing. To separate these two dynamics we will use two-stage least squares (2SLS) regression, a method for estimating models in which the dependent variable *affects*—and is not just affected by—an independent variable.[19] Unfortunately, this method can only be used for House candidates.[20]

The 2SLS results (table 3.10) suggest that there is indeed a two-way relationship between self-financing and party support, specifically that self-financing affects party support and candidates do seem to compensate for weak party support by self-financing. Figure 3.8 depicts the contrast between the *net relationship* between self-financing and party support, suggested by the regular regression, and the *marginal effect* of self-financing on party support, suggested by the 2SLS analysis. Among Democratic House candidates, self-financing $100,000 reduces party support by an average of $388 (although this coefficient is not statistically distinguishable from zero). The *net* relationship between self-financing and party support was a $591 reduction in party support for each $100,000, so part of that "reduction" indeed seems instead to be an *increase* in self-financing in response to low party spending. Among Republican House candidates, self-financing less than $1.4 million seems to attract much more party support—about $19,000 per $100,000 self-financed—than was initially apparent. This effect was probably masked by those candidates who dipped into personal funds when they realized party help would not be forthcoming.

19. The estimation method is very similar to the two-stage process used earlier in this chapter except the coefficients in the second stage explicitly represent the effect of self-financing, not "anticipated" self-financing. The coefficient estimates for *self-financing* and *anticipated self-financing* would actually be identical, but the standard errors (and thus *t*-statistics and *p*-values) would be different.

20. As was noted earlier, information about Senate candidates' wealth and income is unavailable so we do not have useful instrumental variables to use in the first-stage regression. Other potential instruments, such as *early self-financing* and *previous self-financing*, which were used to calculated *anticipated primary self-financing*, do not explain enough variation in *maximum self-financing* among Senate candidates to produce good 2SLS estimates.

TABLE 3.10.   2SLS Regression: Party Support for Potentially Competitive House Nonincumbents in House General Elections, by Party

	House Democrats	House Republicans
Maximum self-financing (two-year cycle)	−387.39	
	(0.69)	
Maximum self-financing, up to "turning point"		18,958.27
		(1.54)
Maximum self-financing, in excess of "turning point"		−16,731.50
		(0.71)
Limit on party coordinated expenditures	1.15	1.92
	(2.02)★	(3.82)★★
Open seat	15,312.14	15,748.33
	(3.91)★★	(2.63)★★
Elective experience	2,180.83	−7,485.22
	(0.48)	(0.68)
Normal party vote	114.47	−125.78
	(0.52)	(0.37)
Previous nominee's margin	396.15	1,066.80
	(2.05)★	(3.28)★★
Freshman opponent (challengers only)	7,497.55	3,586.53
	(2.23)★	(0.57)
Green/Krasno quality score	1,922.67	5,211.65
	(1.72)†	(2.11)★
1994	6,952.20	20,835.54
	(0.81)	(2.54)★
1996	4,677.98	8,590.83
	(0.52)	(1.12)
1998	−3,214.22	—[a]
	(0.32)	
2000	−5,428.03	−49,443.72
	(0.63)	(3.72)★★
Cook's forecast	−6,267.36	−578.11
	(4.13)★★	(0.20)
Same party as retiring incumbent (open seats only)	−9,238.64	−10,190.70
	(1.48)	(0.84)
Constant	−24,987.65	−92,721.44
	(1.47)	(3.17)★★
Observations	525	580
Turning point		$1,499,253

Note: Robust t-statistics (two-tailed) in parentheses
† $p < .10$ ★ $p < .05$ ★★ $p < .01$ ★★★ $p < .001$
[a] 1998 omitted due to multicollinearity

DISCUSSION

This chapter highlights an important aspect of personal spending by political candidates: self-financing impacts elections indirectly by influencing the strategic decisions of other political actors. This impact is apparent in the self-financer's own race, when potential opponents opt out

(A) Republican House Candidates

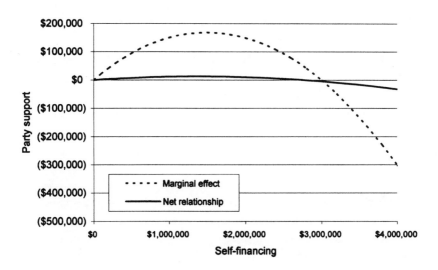

(B) Democratic House Candidates

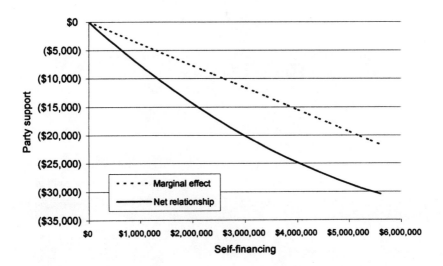

Fig. 3.8. Comparison of marginal effect of *maximum self-financing* on *party support* to net relationship between *maximum self-financing* and *party support*, by party

of contention, and in other contests, when party organizations reallocate funds across races.

The first part of this chapter presented two general findings that clarify the influence of personal spending on the competitive field. Most important, anticipation of a candidate's self-financing *does* deter experienced politicians from entering House races *if* the potential self-financer is running in an open-seat contest. Despite this deterrent effect, self-financing in primary elections is positively correlated with the quality of primary opposition. That is to say, the more a candidate has self-financed, the more experienced opponents he is likely to face. This is not because personal spending in primaries *attracts* experienced opponents; to the contrary, the expectation of self-financing discourages potential candidates with experience in elective office from entering contests. Rather, it is likely that experienced opposition spurs increased self-financing. In other words, experienced candidates are less likely to run when there is a potential self-financer in the race; when they *do* run, they force the potential self-financer to become an actual self-financer, and consequently they face more personal spending than low-quality candidates.

In Senate elections self-financing is also positively correlated with opposition quality; unfortunately, it is impossible to break that relationship down into its component parts, the effect of self-financing on opposition quality and the effect of opposition quality on self-financing. Still, anecdotal evidence clearly identifies instances in which Senate self-financers have either cleared the field, like Michael Huffington, or intimidated a potential rival, like Jon Corzine, whose wealth deterred the congressman widely regarded as the strongest contender from entering a U.S. Senate race. There are also reasons to think that the relative advantage of personal wealth is greater in Senate races. Given the larger scale of Senate campaigns a monetary advantage is presumably more valuable than in a House election. There are also indications that campaigns (and consequently the money that pays for them) simply matter more in Senate elections. Incumbency and the partisan context are more important in House races, where voters have limited knowledge of the candidates; Senate elections are more centered on the individual candidates (Krasno 1994). These factors all suggest that self-financing should have a more powerful deterrent effect in Senate elections.

The deterrent effect of self-financing has two implications for the democratic process. First, it impacts primary election outcomes. The fewer experienced primary opponents a candidate faces, the more likely she is to win the party nomination. Self-financing thus has an indirect effect on primary outcomes, through shaping the opposition, in addition to the potential direct effect, through expenditures. In a sense, open-seat candidates who have the potential to self-finance enjoy a head start even before they have spent their first dollar, since opponents anticipate that spending and, in some cases, bow out of competition. Second, the chilling effect reduces the number of high-quality alternatives among which voters may choose. Jacobson and Kernell introduced the dichotomous elective experience variable by equating "politically experienced" with "well-qualified" (1983, 21), but since then scholars using the "candidate quality" concept have almost universally meant quality as a candidate, not quality as a potential representative.[21] But candidates' primary significance in the political world is as prospective officeholders, so one should not overlook their qualifications and their potential to serve capably in office.

To be clear, the relationships and effects identified do not appear to sway huge numbers of elections. But political scientists, policymakers, and public advocates alike have a strong interest in quantifying the effect of money on election outcomes, and to do so requires an accurate assessment of a multitude of interacting dynamics.

Finally, we saw that party organizations, like potential candidates, tailor their political strategies to some degree in response to self-financing. It is interesting that the spending patterns of the Republicans and the Democrats with respect to self-financing are somewhat different. The Republican Party tends to increase its support for candidates as they self-finance more until personal spending reaches an extreme level, at which point party support falls off. The Democrats, in contrast, tend to let self-financers fend for themselves. The parties' different spending patterns reflect different strategic assessments about moderate self-financing: Republicans appear to see it as an indicator of a good campaign investment, and Democrats generally do not. An interesting question that was not explored here is what these different evaluations tell us about the differences between Democrats and Republicans. Do the leaders of each party simply think about electoral politics differently, such that they use different criteria for funding their nominees? Or are Republican self-financers somehow different than Democratic self-financers in a way that makes them

---

21. The sole exception I have found is from Stone and Maisel (1998). For a review of the candidate quality concept in the political science literature, see the essay entitled "Candidates, Political Quality, and Self-Financing" (Steen 1997).

more "worthy" of party spending? Or do the spending patterns reflect different constraints on the two major parties? Perhaps the Republicans' traditional advantage in "hard money" (money that can be spent to advocate the election or defeat of federal candidates) gave them the luxury of funding moderate self-financers, and Democrats would have done the same if they had more hard money at hand.

This chapter has established that personal spending both responds to and affects the political context in which self-financers seek office. Now that the role of self-financing in a dynamic political environment is better understood we turn our attention to the direct effect of self-financing on financial competition and election outcomes.

CHAPTER 4

How Much Bang in a Self-Financed Buck?

W E HAVE SEEN THAT SELF-FINANCING affects the lineup in election contests, but once the players take the field self-financing can have a more direct effect on competition and election outcomes. Is the game a mismatch from the outset? An election between candidates with vastly disparate campaign treasuries may not be much of a contest. As Joseph Schumpeter notes, the "competitive struggle for the people's vote" is the linchpin of the democratic process ([1942] 1947, 269). Self-financing—especially in large amounts—has the potential to create such disparity between opposing candidates' ability to communicate to voters that the "competitive struggle" becomes a trouncing in which the voters do not have a solid foundation of information upon which to base their decisions. Self-financing may instead—or also—be used more benignly, to make candidates viable when they would otherwise be unable to compete financially. This chapter begins by exploring the balance of financial competition between self-financers and their opponents.

Financial advantage may not always translate into political advantage, so one must also consider the bottom line, the Election Day tally. Do self-financers win more than their fair share of congressional elections? If not, why not? If so, is it because self-financing gives them a significant leg up, or because they run under conditions that would favor any candidate? One cannnot automatically infer that candidates who self-finance generously and win congressional seats have "bought their elections" because other factors, such as bearing the label of the favored party in the district or facing an incompetent opponent, may play the deciding role. Senator Mitch McConnell, the self-proclaimed Darth Vader of campaign finance reform, articulated this concept aptly in his response to Jon Corzine's Democratic primary victory. "The story in New Jersey," McConnell told CNN's Wolf Blitzer, "is that [Corzine] spent $30 million to beat Jim Florio. I mean, that's like the Lakers having to go into double overtime to beat the New Jersey Nets" (Blitzer et al. 2000). McConnell's point, that Corzine owed his primary victory more to former Governor Florio's unpopularity than to his own exorbitant spending, should not be discounted despite McConnell's failure to anticipate that the perennially hapless Nets would challenge the Lakers in the following year's NBA Championship!

One must also be careful not to underestimate the power of personal spending. There are numerous examples of wealthy candidates who self-financed liberally only to lose on Election Day, some by wide margins. Yet one should not conclude from these failed efforts that self-financing is pointless. Texas Democrat Tony Sanchez's $60 million may not have carried him into the governor's mansion in 2002, but it is difficult to imagine *any* Democrat winning that election given the partisan climate in Texas. California Republican Michael Huffington did not win a U.S. Senate seat after self-financing $25 million in his 1994 campaign, but he came within 150,000 votes of unseating a popular incumbent (Dianne Feinstein) in a Democratic state despite his own somewhat underwhelming credentials. As these examples suggest, in evaluating the electoral advantage to self-financing one needs to consider the comparative baseline of how individual self-financers would have fared without personal spending. This task is taken up in the second part of this chapter.

SELF-FINANCING AND FINANCIAL COMPETITIVENESS

Some contests are truly one-sided. In 61 percent of potentially competitive primaries from 1992 through 2000 only one candidate actively offered him- or herself as a "choice."[1] Personal spending (or really the anticipation thereof) has a chilling effect on candidate emergence, as seen in the previous chapter. It is thus possible that some of these elections were uncontested because self-financing intimidated would-be opponents. However, the lone candidate was an extreme self-financer in only 27 one-sided

1. The denominator of this percentage does not include 508 primaries in which no candidate actively campaigned. Obviously these primaries were uncompetitive, but they were "no-sided," not one-sided.

races (3 percent of the total),[2] most of which were out-party challenges in states or districts in which the incumbent's party was strongly favored. It thus seems unlikely that the chilling effect is cold enough to freeze out competition entirely, with a very small number of possible exceptions. Our focus here is on *contested* elections among two or more candidates.

In the worst-case self-financing scenario one candidate uses personal funds to monopolize political discourse. If one candidate drowns out competing voices altogether, the election cannot truly serve as the vehicle by which citizens express their preferences among alternatives. Gloria Ochoa, who lost a House bid to Michael Huffington in 1992, decried "the notion that someone can hit [the voters] with information—whether it be positive or negative—with such frequency and such impact to brainwash them into voting for them" (Miller and Morris 1992). Clearly, this is not how democracy should function ideally. But how commonly do wealthy candidates exploit their financial advantage to such an extent that the democratic ideal of debate between candidates is transmogrified into a monologue? Of course, personal spending may also be used to level the playing field. In contested elections self-financing can make the difference between nominal competition and actual competition.

Trouncers, Competitors, and Trouncees

Let us classify candidates in contested elections as *trouncers, competitors,* and *trouncees* by comparing each candidate's own funding level to that of his or her best-funded rival. The trouncers include anyone whose funding was more than three times his or her leading rival's, trouncees' funding totaled less than one-third of their leading rival's, and competitors include anyone who is neither a trouncer nor a trouncee. For example, in 1998 there were four Republican candidates in California's Third District. Extreme self-financer Doug Ose had the most primary election funding, $1,063,899, and Barbara Alby had the second-most primary funding, $221,958. Because Ose had more than three times as much funding as Alby he is a trouncer. Not all trouncers win and not all trouncees lose, but these categories provide a reasonable indicator of the financial competitiveness

2. Because a candidate who has warded off opposition with threatened self-financing does not have to actually self-finance if he is unopposed in the primary, extreme self-financers in this instance are defined by their self-financing in the entire election cycle.

TABLE 4.1.   Trouncers and Competitors in Actively Contested Primaries, by Self-Financing Level

Elections in which . . .		No Moderate or Extreme Self-Financer in the Race	Moderate or Extreme Self-Financer Was Financial Competitor	Moderate or Extreme Self-Financer was Trouncer	Total
no candidate had three times as much funding as nearest rival	N	168	158		326
	Row %	51.6%	48.4%		100.0%
	Col. %				78.2%
one candidate had three times as much funding as nearest rival	N	59		32	91
	Row %	64.8%		35.2%	100.0%
	Col. %				21.8%

in each primary without having to judge the nuances of every contest individually.[3]

For each actively contested primary one can note whether any candidate trounced his rivals financially and, if so, whether that candidate was a moderate or extreme self-financer. If no candidate enjoyed a huge financial advantage, one can note whether any of the financially competitive candidates were moderate or extreme self-financers. This tabulation, presented in table 4.1, gives a preliminary indication of the role self-financing plays in enhancing or undermining the balance of campaign activity. First note that trouncers are uncommon, found in only 22 percent of actively contested primaries. Moderate and extreme self-financers constitute a significant chunk, 35 percent, of the trouncers, but most trouncers do not rely on personal funds. Self-financing is more prevalent in financially competitive primaries, with 48 percent involving a moderate or extreme self-financer. Not surprisingly, no extreme or moderate self-financer has been financially trounced by his or her opponents.

For those trouncers who do self-finance one must ask, Are their personal funds responsible for their tremendous financial advantage, or would they be able to swamp their opponents with contributions alone? Similarly, does self-financing make any candidates financially competitive, or would their campaign contributions alone keep them in range? Let us imagine an alternate world for each candidate in which the candidate self-

---

3. It is possible for a candidate to be trounced even if there is no trouncer in the race. For example, in the 1996 GOP Georgia Senate race, Paul Collins reported funding of only $145,685 and so was financially trounced by three other candidates, all of whom had more than three times as much money as Collins but none of whom had three times as much as *all* the others.

TABLE 4.2.   Trouncers and Competitors in an Alternate World: Active Candidates in Potentially Competitive States and Districts, Contested House and Senate Primaries

	N	Percentage
Candidate would not have trounced without self-financing.	30	2.6
Candidate would not have been financially competitive without self-financing.	139	12.2
Candidate's self-financing did not affect status.	974	85.2
Total	1,143	100.0

financed nothing. One cannot know how much each candidate would have raised if they had not self-financed—some candidates might have hustled to compensate with additional contributions, while some might have seen their stock fall in the eyes of strategic donors like PAC officials and party leaders and thus lost financial support. Neither can one know exactly how much opponents would have raised and spent—some might have felt less pressure to keep up the arms race, but some might have found it easier to raise money without a self-financed front-runner. However, let us assume that the individual candidate's self-financing is the only thing that changed in her alternate world; all other aspects of the campaign were identical, including her opponents' funding.

Table 4.2 summarizes the differences between the real world and the alternative worlds, revealing that self-financing was more often used to enhance financial competition in primaries than to undermine it. Most trouncers raised enough in contributions to swamp their nearest rivals without self-financing; only 30 candidates (2.6 percent of the total number of candidates) used self-financing to open up a three-to-one financial advantage over their nearest rivals. Most financially competitive candidates would have been financially competitive relying on contributions alone, but 139 candidates (12 percent of the total) would have been trounced without the personal funds they provided to their own campaigns.

When one considers self-financing's impact on general elections it is neither necessary nor advisable to distinguish between pre- and post-primary activity. The benefits a candidate accrues by self-financing in a primary election do not simply vanish if she wins the nomination. Name recognition, favorable impressions, and commitments from primary voters have persistent positive effects because the primary electorate is a part of the general electorate. And some primary publicity reaches members of the other party who are not rigid straight-ticket voters. For these reasons this chapter uses the maximum amount of candidate contributions and net loans in a two- or six-year cycle (*total self-financing*) to measure self-financing for general elections.[4]

As in primaries, self-financing by nominees is used more to mitigate imbalances than to create them. The pattern is more pronounced in general elections because most opponents are incumbent representatives or senators whose fund-raising prowess makes them difficult to overwhelm financially. As table 4.3 illustrates, incumbents are less likely to trounce their general election opponents when their opponents are moderate or extreme self-financers. When the challenger self-financed less than $50,000 (the minimum for moderate self-financers), nearly half of incumbents (48.3 percent) trounced their opponents, outspending them by more than three-to-one; in contrast, when the challenger self-financed $50,000 or more, only about a quarter of incumbents (26.2 percent) trounced their opponents. In open seats self-financing was also used more often to make candidates competitive (74 elections) than to trounce opponents (only 16 elections). Trounces were slightly less likely to occur when a moderate or extreme self-financer was involved in an open-seat general election (17.8 percent of elections, compared to 21.9 percent of elections without a moderate or extreme self-financer).

For the vast majority of general-election candidates, self-financing did not affect their status as trouncers, competitors, or trouncees. Table 4.4 summarizes the comparison between candidates' actual status and the status they would have held had they not self-financed. Only nine trouncers (.8 percent of all candidates who self-financed at least one dollar)—all in open seats—would not have been able to swamp their opponents without personal funds. In contrast, 95 financial competitors (9.0 percent of all self-financing candidates, most of them challengers) used self-financing to pull within financial range of their opponents. In other words, these candidates would have been financially overwhelmed had they not used personal funds in their campaigns. However, for 90 percent of general-election candidates who self-financed at all, self-financing did not materially affect the balance of competition.

With respect to the balance of financial competition there are clearly pros and cons to self-financing. Sometimes self-financing makes primaries and open-seat contests less competitive, when a candidate self-finances so

---

4. In chapter 2 I used *general-election self-financing*, which excluded preprimary financial activity, because I was exploring the incentives to self-finance and those incentives change once a candidate wins nomination.

TABLE 4.3.   Trouncers and Financial Competitors in General Elections

A.   Challenges

	No Moderate or Extreme Self-Financer in the Race	Challenger was Moderate or Extreme Self-Financer	Total
Incumbent did not trounce	304	127	430
Row %	70.7%	29.5%	100.0%
Col. %	51.7%	73.8%	56.6%
Incumbent trounced challenger	284	45	329
Row %	86.3%	13.7%	100.0%
Col. %	48.3%	26.2%	43.3%
All challenges	588	172	760
Row %	77.4%	22.6%	100.0%
Col. %	100.0%	100.0%	100.0%

B.   Open Seats

	No Moderate or Extreme Self-Financer was Financial Competitor or Trouncer	Moderate or Extreme Self-Financer was Financial Competitor or Trouncer	Total
No candidate had three times as much funding as nearest rival			
N	89	74	163
Row %	54.6%	45.4%	100.0%
Col. %	78.1%	82.2%	79.9%
One candidate had three times as much funding as nearest rival			
N	25	16	41
Row %	61.0%	39.0%	100.0%
Col. %	21.9%	17.8%	20.1%
All open-seat elections			
N	114	90	204
Row %	55.9%	44.1%	100.0%
Col. %	100.0%	100.0%	100.0%

much that the opponent (or opponents) are overwhelmed, but more often self-financing plays a more benign role—from the perspective of democratic theorists if not incumbents—helping candidates to make themselves heard without drowning out the opposition. It may be cold comfort to self-financers' opponents, especially the ones who get swamped by personal spending, but self-financing provides value to democracy when it increases the number of viable options in an election.

TABLE 4.4.   Trouncers and Competitors in an Alternative World (general elections)

		Challengers	Open–Seat Candidates	Total
Candidate would not have trounced	N	0	9	9
without self-financing.	Col. %	0.0%	3.0%	.8%
Candidate would not have been financially	N	76	19	95
competitive without self-financing.	Col. %	10.1%	6.2%	9.0%
Candidate's self-financing did not affect	N	681	380	1,061
status.	Col. %	89.9%	90.8%	90.2%
Total		757	408	1,165

SELF-FINANCING AND ELECTORAL ADVANTAGE

A candidate's chance of winning a primary or general election tends to *decrease* as the amount of personal funds invested in their campaigns increases (chap. 1). The unimpressive track record posted by deep-pocketed candidates seems initially to contradict a large body of empirical evidence presented by political scientists. Scholars agree that campaign spending has a positive impact on challengers' vote tallies (Abramowitz 1991; Gerber 1998; Goidel and Gross 1994; Green and Krasno 1988, 1990; Jacobson 1978, 1985, 1990; Kenny and McBurnett 1994), so it seems reasonable to expect that candidates with a built-in funding source would do better than those without. However, this built-in funding has been remarkably ineffective at securing election victories.

This does not necessarily mean that self-financing is not a political advantage, or that self-financing somehow causes candidates to lose elections. Self-financing candidates might very well have won even fewer races had they self-financed less or not at all. Alas, one cannot run a "do-over" of every election to test this hypothesis directly; one can, however, compare similarly situated candidates to see whether those who self-financed attracted more votes than those who didn't. Consider, for example, one of the most important determinants of a candidate's success: whether or not she was opposed. More than one-quarter of all non-self-financers were unopposed for their party's nomination and thus guaranteed a primary victory, while only 3 percent of extreme self-financers were unopposed in the primary. If one only considers candidates in actively contested primaries, victory rates still tend to decrease with self-financing but not as much as they do when primary opposition is not held constant (fig. 4.1).

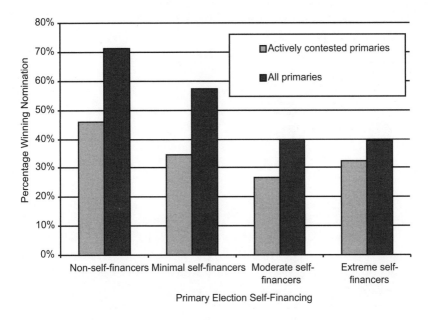

Fig. 4.1. Victory rates in primary elections, by self-financing level

One could continue dividing candidates into groups with similar characteristics. However, given the number of political variables that influence both vote tallies it would not take long before each group contained only one candidate! A more practical approach is to use multivariate regression techniques to estimate the effect of self-financing on vote margins and election outcomes when other political variables are held constant.

A Model of Vote Margins

A candidate's actual vote tally and his probability of winning the election can be conceptualized as functions of his support in the electorate plus a random component that represents completely unpredictable influences, such as the distribution of voters who make mistakes in marking their ballots or the distribution of would-be voters who are prevented unexpectedly from voting.[5] Support in the electorate, in turn, is determined by characteristics of the candidate, features of the district, national political

5. The aftermath of the 2000 presidential vote in Florida indicates that machine reading of ballots also contributes to random variation in vote tallies.

conditions, and the nature of the campaigns. Algebraically this model can thus be represented as:

$$vote\ margin = XB + \varepsilon. \tag{4.1}$$

X signifies the determinants of the election and B is a vector of coefficients, the marginal effects of each variable on the vote margin. The randomness inherent in every vote tally is represented by ε.

Some variables in X, such as self-financing and fundraising, are fairly easy to identify and measure. Others, however, simply cannot be measured. These unmeasurable variables represent idiosyncratic aspects of each contest such as local endorsements, gaffes committed by one candidate, an especially popular or unpopular vote cast by the incumbent, or an unusually charismatic candidate. These idiosyncrasies can have a significant impact on election results but are very difficult, perhaps even impossible, to measure. However, one cannot just ignore them. If any omitted variable is significantly correlated with an included variable, its effect on the vote will essentially be incorporated into the coefficient for the included variable. The true marginal effect of the included variable would thus be obscured.

There are statistical methods that eliminate (or at least reduce) omitted-variable bias, but before forging ahead with a complicated method one should consider whether omitted-variable bias seems like a serious problem in this situation. Are the unmeasurable variables significantly correlated with the included variables? Indeed, there are reasons to suspect that the answer is yes.

Any political condition that increases a candidate's electoral support should also increase her ability to attract campaign contributions (Goidel and Gross 1994; Green and Krasno 1988, 1990; Jacobson 1978, 1985; Welch 1981). As Bruce Cain notes, "Good standing in the polls generates expectations of success, which in turn encourages donors to contribute to the campaign" (1995, 253). Imagine, for example, the ramifications of an October surprise—say, revelations that the incumbent congressman beat his wife, sold crack to kids, and allowed a lobbyist to buy him a cup of coffee at the Cannon Carry-Out. Many voters would choose the challenger solely on the basis of this news. Many strategic contributors would offer new financial support, recognizing both the opportunity to sway the outcome and the possibility that the challenger would become the new guy to see on Capitol Hill. Political scientists' theories are echoed by political consultants, whose personal involvement in individual campaigns allows them to observe the idiosyncrasies that cannot be systematically coded. For example, David Bienstock, a consultant to California governor Pete Wilson's reelection campaign in 1994, made the following observation about Wilson's Democratic opponent, state treasurer Kathleen Brown: "Major Democratic contributors smelled a loss, and they just shut their wallets" (Lubenow 1995, 254).

Some scholars have also argued that incumbents' fund-raising is positively correlated with elite expectations favoring the challenger (Green and Krasno 1988; Goidel and Gross 1994; Jacobson 1978, 1990). That is to say, incumbents can raise virtually unlimited amounts, but since they have other priorities and dislike fund-raising they only raise as much as they think is necessary. When their challengers are doing quite well, incumbents step up their fund-raising efforts. This dynamic is often credited for the counterintuitive positive relationship between incumbent fund-raising and challenger vote margins found in many studies.

If self-financing is driven in part by an inability to raise sufficient funds, idiosyncratic factors that contribute to one candidate's success should also decrease that candidate's need to self-finance. Recall the finding in chapter 2 that extreme self-financers ratchet up self-financing in the final weeks of their campaigns, suggesting that self-financing indeed responds to elements in the strategic environment. It was also shown that self-financing in primaries varied with local conditions. It is thus reasonable to think that self-financing totals are influenced by late-breaking developments in a campaign.

Because it is likely that the variables *total contributions, total self-financing, opponent's contributions,* and *opponent's self-financing* are all significantly correlated with unmeasurable variables it is advisable to use two-stage least squares regression (2SLS), a method that reduces the bias in coefficient estimates when confounding variables are not explicitly included in an equation. The first stage of 2SLS regresses the endogenous variables, *total contributions, total self-financing, opponent's contributions,* and *opponent's self-financing,* on the exogenous independent variables and a vector of instrumental variables. Each instrumental variable is correlated with an endogenous regressor but does not have a significant independent relationship with the election outcome. The predicted values of the endogenous variables produced by the first-stage regressions are highly correlated with the original variables but have essentially been purged of correlation with the confounding "October surprises." The second stage uses the first-stage predictions as instruments for the endogenous variables in the original equations. If one has exogenous instruments for all of the endogenous variables in an equation, 2SLS produces unbiased coefficient estimates. In this case, as is discussed in appendix C, the instruments for *contributions* are not wholly exogenous. Consequently, omitted-variable bias is reduced but not eliminated entirely.

Instruments for *total self-financing* include three variables coded from candidates' Personal Financial Disclosure statements filed with the Clerk of the House of Representatives: *previous year's unearned income, previous year's earned income,* and *value of assets in previous year.* The amount each candidate reported in his or her first disclosure, *early contributions,* is used as an instrument for *total contributions.*

Unfortunately, information on Senate candidates' personal wealth is no longer available for past election cycles. Neither are there adequate instruments for the variable *contributions* in primary elections. It is impossible to use 2SLS to analyze primary elections or Senate campaigns, so we shall proceed with analysis of general elections for the U.S. House of Representatives and then consider the likely implications of the findings for primaries and Senate elections.

General Elections

Two-stage least squares regression is performed separately on four groups of candidates: inexperienced challengers, experienced challengers, inexperienced open-seat candidates, and experienced open-seat candidates. This allows one to discover whether there are notable differences in how self-financing affects vote tallies depending on key characteristics of the candidate.

The regression equation is designed to compare the effects of self-financing and fund-raising, so the two primary variables for each candidate are *self-financing* and *contributions.* The control variables include indicators of the local partisan context (*normal party vote* and *previous nominee's margin,* candidate in *same party as retiring incumbent*), measures of the relative quality of the candidates (*Green and Krasno's candidate-quality score, opponent's elective experience, opponent's candidate-quality score,* whether candidate is a *freshman incumbent, opponent's funding,* and, for open-seat candidates, *opponent's self-financing*), and indicators of national conditions favoring one party (one dummy variable for each combination of political party and election cycle). Of course candidate experience and seat status are held constant by calculating separate coefficients for each of the four groups.

The statistical results, listed in table 4.5, suggest that self-financing has a smaller effect on vote margins than campaign contributions do. The first row lists b_{SF}, the coefficients of *self-financing* in each sample, and the second row lists b_{FR}, the coefficients of *contributions*. The difference between the two coefficients is listed in the third row along with the corresponding *t*-ratios. In all four groups the coefficient of self-financing (b_{SF}) is positive, and in both groups of open-seat candidates it is statistically significant, indicating that self-financing does have a positive marginal effect on candidates' vote totals. Indeed, it would be quite surprising to find otherwise. However, b_{SF} is smaller than b_{FR} in three of the four groups (the exception is experienced challengers), and the difference is statistically significant in all three groups. In other words, it appears that self-financing has a smaller impact on candidates' vote totals than campaign contributions do. Explanations for and implications of this very interesting finding will be considered at length later in this chapter.

The coefficients in table 4.5 provide a very crude indicator of the effect of self-financing and contributions on vote margins. Each coefficient essentially represents the *average* effect of $100,000 in self-financing or contributions, but not the marginal effect of any single increment of $100,000. The marginal effect of $100,000 is likely to be greatest when no other funds are expended. Because, as Jacobson notes, "no candidate can get more than 100 percent of the vote, no matter how much is spent" (1978, 471), once a candidate has spent, say, $2 million, spending another $100,000 is not likely to sway anyone in most situations. One can thus conclude that on average a $100,000 increase in self-financing adds .5 percentage points to an inexperienced open-seat candidate's vote margin but not, for example, that inexperienced open-seat candidates who self-finance exactly $100,000 increase their vote margins by an average of .5 percentage points. If one wants to more accurately describe the effect of different levels of personal funding, one must account for diminishing marginal effects. Failing to account for a diminishing marginal effect can also result in over- or underestimation of the difference between self-financing and contributions (appendix D).

It is common for scholars to transform funding variables using the natural logarithm; however, this is an arbitrary choice and may misstate marginal effects as much as using untransformed dollars. No one really knows for sure the rate at which the effect of campaign funding declines or whether that rate is about the same for different kinds of candidates in different kinds of political situations. Still, there are clues hidden in the data themselves. One can estimate separate coefficients for different ranges of

TABLE 4.5. **2SLS Regression: Vote Margins of Active Nonincumbent Candidates in Potentially Competitive House Elections**

	Open Seats, No Experience	Open Seats, Experience	Challengers, No Experience	Challengers, Experience
Self-financing	0.5	0.5	0.3	1.3
	(2.38)*	(2.38)*	(0.72)	(0.96)
Contributions	1.8	1.8	2.4	1.0
	(2.79)**	(3.14)**	(5.94)**	(2.41)*
(Contributions − self-financing)	0.4	1.3	2.12	−0.2
	(1.94)*	(2.66)**	(3.93)**	(0.17)
Opponent's self-financing	0.7	1.4		
	(1.56)	(3.09)**		
Opponent's funding	−1.0	−2.0	−0.3	−0.2
	(1.84)†	(4.10)**	(0.99)	(0.49)
Normal party vote	1.3	0.9	0.3	0.4
	(4.30)**	(4.65)**	(2.79)**	(3.09)**
Previous nominee's vote	0.0	−0.1	0.4	0.5
	(0.02)	(0.88)	(4.10)**	(4.22)**
Same party as retiring incumbent	5.1	4.0		
	(1.23)	(1.30)		
Opponent's experience	4.6	0.9		
	(1.24)	(0.43)		
Green/Krasno score	0.8	2.1	1.0	1.1
	(0.84)	(1.95)†	(2.09)*	(1.17)
Democrat—1994	−34.3	−39.8	−44.1	−52.2
	(2.43)*	(4.48)**	(6.55)**	(4.54)**
Democrat—1996	−11.0	−6.5	−8.6	−6.2
	(0.91)	(0.54)	(1.40)	(0.73)
Democrat—1998	5.3	−8.2	−16.8	−17.0
	(0.35)	(0.76)	(2.40)*	(1.75)†
Democrat—2000	14.1	−7.0	−18.0	−24.4
	(0.94)	(0.60)	(2.73)**	(2.68)**
Republican—1992	−6.5	−8.9	3.0	−0.5
	(0.82)	(2.43)*	(0.92)	(0.10)
Republican—1994	21.9	27.6	15.6	22.3
	(3.02)**	(6.52)**	(4.52)**	(3.91)**
Republican—1996	5.7	6.5	−8.8	−8.9
	(0.80)	(1.12)	(2.25)*	(1.83)†
Republican—1998	−5.3	6.7	−4.8	−3.6
	(0.62)	(1.19)	(1.29)	(0.72)
Republican—2000	−14.4	7.0	−4.8	−0.3
	(1.65)	(1.27)	(1.23)	(0.07)
Freshman incumbent			1.9	−0.6
			(1.43)	(0.33)
Constant	6.7	5.1	−24.2	−19.4
	(0.57)	(0.68)	(4.47)**	(2.38)*
Observations	141	183	491	266

Note: t-statistics in parentheses; standard errors adjusted to reflect clustering of observations within unique primary elections.
† $p < .10$ * $p < .05$;   ** $p < .01$ *** $p < .001$

funding, then select a transformation that smooths out the patterns (which to the naked eye can look more like chicken scratch than systematic patterns) suggested by the coefficients. Doing so suggests that an appropriate transformation for nonincumbent funding is:

$$f(total\ funding) = \frac{(total\ self\text{-}financing + total\ contributions)^{.50} - 1}{.50}.$$

For incumbent funding the transformation is:

$$f(total\ funding) = \frac{(total\ self\text{-}financing + total\ contributions)^{3.7} - 1}{3.7}.^{6}$$

(See appendix E for details on the selection of these two functions.) Because self-financing is seemingly less productive than campaign contributions, the diminishing-marginal-effects model also includes an interaction term,

percent self-financed $\times f(total\ funding)$,

to indicate how much the effect of campaign funding decreases when it comes from a candidate's own pocket.

Two-stage least squares results for the diminishing-marginal-effects model are presented in table 4.6. The first row lists b_1, the coefficients of $f(total\ self\text{-}financing + total\ contributions)$ in each sample, and the second row lists b_2, the coefficients of *percentage self-financed* $\times f(total\ self\text{-}financing + total\ contributions)$. In all four groups, the coefficient b_2 is negative, suggesting that the effect of campaign funds does decrease as the percentage of total funds self-financed increases. In other words, the difference between fund-raising and self-financing initially identified is not explained away by diminishing marginal returns to campaign funding. b_2 is statistically significant in two of the four groups.

Because of the diminishing-marginal-effects transformation, the coefficients do not represent the increase in vote margin resulting from a fixed increase in funding. The marginal effect of $1, $50,000, or any other

---

6. Interestingly, the transformation for incumbents suggests an *increasing* marginal effect. This may indicate that incumbent expenditures do not have much effect unless or until they are very large.

TABLE 4.6. 2SLS Regression: Vote Margins of Active Nonincumbent Candidates in Potentially Competitive House Elections—Diminishing Marginal Effect Model

	Open Seats, No Experience	Open Seats, Experience	Challengers, No Experience	Challengers, Experience
f(total funding)	3.9	4.2	4.8	2.7
	(2.79)★★	(3.46)★★	(6.43)★★	(1.54)
Percentage SF'ed × f(total funding)	−2.2	−2.3	−4.6	−1.1
	(1.29)	(2.76)★★	(3.51)★★	(0.23)
f(total funding) − opponent	−2.6	−4.6	0.0	0.0
	(2.13)★	(4.40)★★	(1.43)	(0.02)
Percentage SF'ed × f(total funding) − opponent	2.4	2.1		
	(1.86)†	(1.93)†		
Normal party vote	1.2	0.8	0.3	0.4
	(4.09)★★	(4.41)★★	(2.64)★★	(3.07)★★
Previous nominee's vote	0.0	−0.1	0.4	0.4
	(0.11)	(0.52)	(4.00)★★	(3.27)★★
Same party as retiring incumbent	4.4	3.0		
	(1.09)	(1.06)		
Opponent's experience	4.8	1.5		
	(1.32)	(0.74)		
Opponent's Green/Krasno score	−1.0	−0.4		
	(1.24)	(0.73)		
Democrat—1994	−32.5	−40.6	−43.6	−50.2
	(2.35)★	(4.76)★★	(6.76)★★	(4.52)★★
Democrat—1996	−10.3	−7.3	−8.9	−5.8
	(0.88)	(0.64)	(1.52)	(0.71)
Democrat—1998	7.0	−7.0	−17.3	−16.7
	(0.48)	(0.69)	(2.54)★	(1.80)†
Democrat—2000	13.2	−9.6	−17.7	−22.6
	(0.85)	(0.94)	(2.84)★★	(2.33)★
Republican—1992	−5.2	−7.6	2.5	−0.8
	(0.66)	(2.06)★	(0.80)	(0.20)
Republican—1994	20.4	26.7	15.8	22.1
	(2.80)★★	(6.31)★★	(4.80)★★	(4.11)★★
Republican—1996	4.7	5.7	−8.1	−8.3
	(0.68)	(0.99)	(2.24)★	(1.84)†
Republican—1998	−6.3	4.3	−4.1	−2.9
	(0.77)	(0.80)	(1.12)	(0.63)
Republican—2000	−13.1	7.2	−4.4	−0.8
	(1.46)	(1.60)	(1.26)	(0.15)
Freshman incumbent			1.2	−0.9
			(0.88)	(0.51)
Constant	4.9	4.7	−22.8	−18.1
	(0.42)	(0.68)	(4.30)★★	(2.42)★
Observations	141	183	491	266

Note: t-statistics in parentheses; standard errors adjusted to reflect clustering of observations within unique primary elections.
† p < .10   ★ p < .05   ★★ p < .01   ★★★ p < .001

amount depends on (1) whether it is raised or self-financed, (2) the base-line amount of self-financing, and (3) the baseline amount of campaign contributions. Because the calculations are complex it is most useful to illustrate the effect of self-financing with pictures. Figure 4.2 contrasts the effect of self-financing when contributions are equal to zero with the effect of contributions when self-financing is equal to zero for each of the four groups.[7]

Panel A of figure 4.2 illustrates the effect of campaign funding for challengers with no experience in elective office. The diminishing marginal effect is clearly apparent in the shape of the curves, and self-financing has very little impact, especially in comparison to fund-raising. For example, self-financing $500,000 improves candidates' margins by an average of less than 1 point (when they raise nothing), while raising $500,000 increases margins by an average of 22 points (when candidates self-finance nothing). For challengers with officeholding experience the gap between fund-raising and self-financing was much narrower (panel B), as self-financing was more productive and contributions were less productive than for inexperienced challengers. Self-financing $500,000 adds an average of 7 points to experienced challengers' vote margins, while raising $500,000 adds an average of 12 points when candidates have no other funds.

Self-financing helps inexperienced open-seat candidates considerably more than inexperienced challengers as panel C of figure 4.2 illustrates, although personal funds still have a notably smaller effect than raised contributions. Self-financing $500,000 increases vote margins by an average of 8 points in this group, and $500,000 in contributions raises margins by an average of 18 points. Self-financing and fund-raising have almost the same effect on vote margins among experienced open-seat candidates as they do for inexperienced open-seat candidates. Providing $500,000 in personal funds to one's own campaign (and raising $0) adds an average of

7. To calculate the predicted effects depicted in the figures I assume that candidates self-finance a constant proportion of campaign funds throughout a campaign. Therefore, the predicted effect of self-financing equals the predicted effect of total funding times the percentage self-financed, or (β_1 + *percentage self-financed* β_2) × *f(total self-financing + total contributions)*. This produces a very different estimated marginal effect than, say, comparing the effect of total funding to the effect of contributions alone, which assumes that all contributions *precede* all self-financing. In fact, we will see later that self-financing tends to precede fund-raising, so the predicted effects depicted in the figures slightly underestimate the true effect of self-financing.

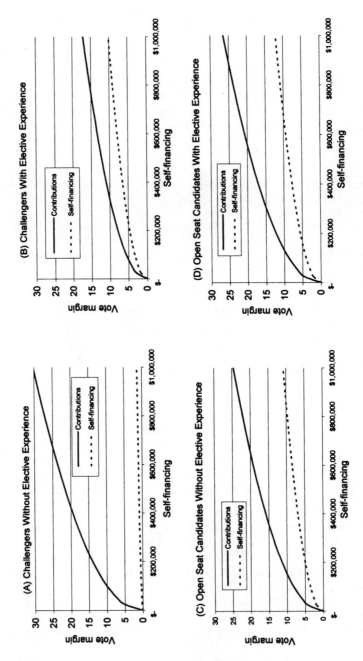

Fig. 4.2. Marginal effect of self-financing compared to marginal effect of contributions, by seat status and candidate experience

9 points to candidate margins, while raising $500,000 from campaign contributors (and self-financing nothing) adds an average of 19 points.

The most striking aspect of figure 4.2 is the aberrance of panel A. In three of the groups the effects of campaign funding are very similar, but among inexperienced challengers the effect of self-financing is remarkably small and the effect of campaign contributions is noticeably large. One might wonder whether this deviation is simply an artifact of outlying cases in the group, but dropping two outliers and reestimating the 2SLS equation produces virtually identical results. However, if one excludes just one candidate from the inexperienced *open-seat* candidates the 2SLS coefficients change significantly such that the effect of self-financing is wiped out entirely. Self-financing by inexperienced open-seat candidates only seems productive because Michael Huffington self-financed more than twice as much as the next-most-generous candidate and won an 18-point victory in 1992 (the seat was open because Huffington had ousted incumbent Representative Bob Lagomarsino in the Republican primary). When Huffington is excluded from the calculations, self-financing by inexperienced open-seat candidates appears just as futile as self-financing by inexperienced challengers.

These results are consistent with the findings in chapter 3, where anticipated self-financing had no effect on opposition quality for inexperienced challengers. Strategic politicians are apparently justified in their failure to be intimated by self-financing among this group, as it has no discernible effect on their vote tallies in general elections. Similarly, self-financing by experienced candidates was found to be more discouraging to potential opponents than self-financing by inexperienced candidates. This conclusion is also bolstered by the results presented here, as self-financing by experienced candidates appears to be more productive than self-financing by inexperienced candidates.

Extreme Self-Financers

The statistics presented in this chapter illuminate the self-financing phenomenon by describing overall patterns that are difficult to discern by examining individual elections. This is at once the advantage and disadvantage of statistics—that they obscure case-by-case variation. However, one should not forget that such individual variation exists. On average, self-financing has little effect on election margins, but there are undoubtedly some candidates who benefited tremendously from their use of personal funds. Huffington is an obvious example—indeed, self-financing helped him so much in 1992 that it pulled up the average effect estimated with 140 other candidates.

There are other specific cases in which it is clear to an intelligent observer that self-financing was an important factor in deciding the outcome, no matter what the statistics say. For example, in 1996 Democratic challenger Ellen Tauscher, a businesswoman who had not previously held elective office, defeated Representative Bill Baker in California's Tenth District. If Tauscher had not self-financed $1.5 million Baker would have handily outspent her and undoubtedly prevailed at the polls. Still, such clear-cut examples are hard to identify. It is much easier to spot extreme self-financers whose margins are easily attributable to other factors. Several extreme self-financers ousted Democratic incumbents in 1994, a year in which Democratic incumbents made easy targets. Consider Frank Cremeans, who narrowly defeated Democratic representative Ted Strickland (by only 1 point) in a district that had strongly favored Republicans and given Strickland less than 50 percent the previous year. Given these local conditions and the national tide favoring Republicans, it is surprising that Cremeans's margin was so small.

Other candidates simply cannot seem to get any political traction with personal spending. Phil Sudan, a Republican lawyer who challenged Representative Ken Bentsen (D-Texas) in 2000, self-financed close to $3 million yet lost by the staggering margin of 21 points. Republican Linda Bean self-financed nearly $1 million in her 1992 campaign against Democratic Representative Tom Andrews (D-Maine), outspending Andrews by almost two to one. The district had favored George Bush in 1988 and went Republican two years later when Andrews ran for Senate, yet Bean still lost by 31 points.

SENATE ELECTIONS

There are reasons to believe that extreme self-financing is more productive in Senate elections than House elections. First, because Senate candidates must appeal to voters across an entire state, Senate campaigns usually cost more than House campaigns. It is thus harder for a Senate candidate than a House candidate to raise enough funds for a viable campaign, which magnifies the relative value of self-financing.

Comparing the victory rates of House and Senate candidates (table 4.7)

TABLE 4.7.   Candidate Election Rates in Primary and General Elections, by Chamber and Self-Financing Level: Active Nonincumbents in Potentially Competitive States and Districts

	Senate		House	
	Winners (%)	N	Winners (%)	N
Non–self-financer ($0)	46	63	34	210
Minimal self-financer ($1–$49,999)	11	54	20	647
Moderate self-financer ($50,000–BCRA threshold)	16	43	21	208
Extreme self-financer (above BCRA threshold)	40	20	31	45
All candidates	28	180	23	1,110

provides some preliminary evidence for this notion. Minimal and moderate self-financers did remarkably poorly in Senate general elections, winning only 11 percent and 16 percent of their elections, compared to 20 percent and 21 percent in House elections. Extreme self-financers did quite well, winning 40 percent of Senate elections, compared to 31 percent of extreme self-financers in House general elections.

For some of the successful extreme self-financers there are explanations for their victories that have little to do with personal spending. Consider, for example, Republican Peter Fitzgerald, who defeated Senator Carol Moseley Braun in the 1998 election. Moseley Braun, who had been dogged by controversy and allegations of ethical breaches, was considered one of the Senate's most vulnerable incumbents. Democratic self-financer Mark Dayton found himself in an analogous position two years later as he faced Senator Rod Grams in Minnesota. Minnesota is competitive for both major parties (and independents too), and Grams, whose margin in the banner Republican year of 1994 was only 6 points, had been plagued by personal scandals and a lackluster campaign.

For other Senate self-financers it is hard to dismiss the role their personal funding played in getting them elected. Regarding Maria Cantwell (D-Washington) one political columnist noted, "Before her financial windfall, no one would have taken Cantwell very seriously as a challenger to GOP Sen. Slade Gorton" (Todd 2000). Even with a strong financial advantage and the Washington state electorate strongly favoring Democratic candidates, Cantwell defeated Gorton by the amazingly narrow margin of 2,229 votes.

Table 4.8 groups extreme self-financers in Senate elections into the familiar four categories by seat status and prior experience and lists the

TABLE 4.8.   Candidate Election Rates in General Elections, by Self-Financing Level:
Active Nonincumbents in Potentially Competitive Senate Elections

	Extreme Self-Financers	Others
Inexperienced open-seat candidates	33%	33%
N	6	
Experienced open-seat candidates	100%	54%
N	1	
Inexperienced challenger	22%	2%
N	9	
Experienced challengers	60%	21%
N	5	

success rates for extreme self-financers and other candidates in the corresponding group. In open Senate seats extreme self-financers perform at about the same level as other candidates, experience held constant. In challenges to incumbent senators, however, extreme self-financers perform extraordinarily well in comparison to other challengers. Senate challengers without previous officeholding experience almost never win elections unless they are extreme self-financers, in which case their group victory rate is 22 percent (two winners out of nine candidates). If there were truly no difference between extreme self-financers and other candidates in this category such that the chance of any single candidate winning were 2 percent (the victory rate exclusive of extreme self-financers), the probability of two or more of the nine self-financers winning would be .008—extremely unlikely. Challengers who had held elective office prior to running for Senate fared significantly better, winning 21 percent of their elections if they were not extreme self-financers, but the extreme self-financers again outperformed their fellow candidates by a wide margin, with three out of five winning. Such a result would be highly improbable ($p = .068$) if there were no underlying difference between extreme self-financers and everyone else. However, one cannot be confident that extreme self-financers' relatively high success rates in Senate elections are not caused by other political factors or simply good luck.

A NOTE ON SELF-FINANCING IN PRIMARIES

This chapter has focused on general elections, but let us not forget that most candidates must clear two hurdles to get elected—a primary first, then a general. Chapter 3 demonstrated one aspect of how self-financing affects primaries, by shaping the field of candidates, but it is difficult to tease out the direct effect of self-financing on primary results. This is largely because the unmeasurable factors shaping the outcomes are surely more significant at the nominating stage when voters do not have party labels to help them distinguish among candidates. Frustrating this inquiry even more, the tools that facilitate isolating the effect of self-financing in general elections are simply not available for primaries. There is no instrumental variable appropriate for purging excluded-variable bias in primary-period contributions. The variable *early contributions,* the instrument used for contributions in general elections, is virtually a proxy for *primary contributions,* especially in states with early primaries. While *early contributions* may itself be slightly correlated with excluded variables in general elections, it is likely to be much more so in primary elections, when the voters' decisions are made not long after early contributions are raised.

Although one cannot make precise estimates about the effect of self-financing in primaries or compare it to fund-raising, it is reasonable to expect funding of any kind to have a greater impact on primary elections than general elections for the very reason that impact is hard to measure. Campaigns simply matter more in primaries (Jacobson 1975, 783). Since party identification is still the most important determinant of vote choice in partisan elections, there is more room in primary elections for campaign activity—self-financed or otherwise—to move voters than in general elections.

THE DIFFERENCE BETWEEN SELF-FINANCING AND FUND-RAISING

The empirical analysis offered in this chapter provides evidence that a dollar self-financed does not equal a dollar raised. In both open-seat races and incumbent challenges, self-financing produces a smaller vote margin than fund-raising does; the difference is especially remarkable among inexperienced candidates. This finding is puzzling—if television stations charge the same rates for self-financed ads and ads funded by contributions, which they do, and if printers do not charge extra for brochures purchased with personal funds, which they do not, why does self-financing buy less support than fund-raising does? The difference is even more mysterious given that self-financing can be deployed on Day One of a candidacy whereas contributions trickle in over the course of a campaign. Gary Jacobson has noted, "In general, money available early in the campaign is put to much better use than money received later. . . . This circumstance adds to the advantage of personal wealth" (1997, 65). Four possible differences between self-financing and fund-raising suggest explanations for the relative ineffectiveness of personal spending: the timing of funding, the relative quality of self-financers and fund-raisers, the process of collecting funds, and the nature of expenditures.

Timing of Campaign Receipts

Political common sense and political science agree that early money is more productive than late spending (Biersack, Herrnson, and Wilcox 1993). Consider, then, a hypothetical scenario in which all candidates always exhaust their raised contributions before committing any personal funds to a race. In this situation one would expect self-financing to have less sway over the outcome dollar-for-dollar than the contributions raised earlier in the cycle.

This seems an unlikely explanation for the actual gap between self-financing and contributions. Chapter 2 presented evidence that most individual candidates understand the value of early spending and thus front-load personal spending. However, we also learned that some candidates indulge in late self-financing sprees. It is thus possible that in the *aggregate* personal funds are expended later than raised contributions. In other words, late self-financing (which should be least productive) may dwarf early self-financing (which should be most productive) when the two are combined.

A simple way to examine the relative timing of aggregate self-financing and aggregate fund-raising is to divide each campaign into the nine Federal Election Commission reporting periods and calculate average self-financing and average fund-raising per day in each time frame. Because candidates enter the fray at different times in an election cycle one should consider funding timing with respect to each candidate's personal time line, ordering the reporting periods relative to the date of entry (not, say, to the first day of the election cycle). Figure 4.3 groups disclosure reports according to the order in which they were filed and depicts the average amounts of self-financing and fund-raising per day in each group. Eyeballing the data presented in figure 4.3, it appears that self-financing and fund-raising tend to follow about the same schedule, although self-financing tends to *precede* fund-raising a bit, as the line representing average self-financing is generally to the left of the line representing average fund-raising.

The eyeball test is confirmed by calculating the average number of days

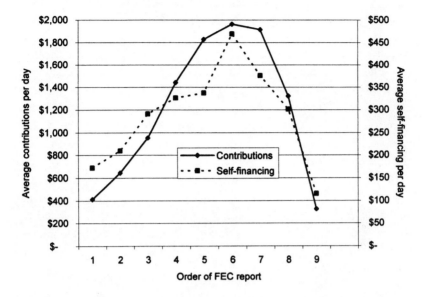

Fig. 4.3.   Average self-financing and contributions per day, by order of FEC report

elapsed since a candidate's entry into the race *per dollar self-financed or raised*. If a candidate only self-finances one dollar and does so after 50 days of campaigning, the average days elapsed per dollar self-financed is 50. If a candidate self-finances $100 after 50 days and another $200 after 65 days, the average days elapsed per dollar is:

($100 × 50 days + $200 × 65 days) / $300 = 60 days.

Using this calculation, the average number-of-days-elapsed-per-dollar is considerably less for self-financing—252 days—than for fund-raising—301 days.[8] This statistic strongly suggests that the weaker impact of self-financing on vote margins is not attributable to the timing of campaign receipts. In fact, self-financing tends to precede fund-raising and should therefore offer more bang for the buck, not less, than fund-raising.

8. Unfortunately I cannot identify the exact date on which each candidate entered a race or the exact date on which each dollar was collected. As an approximation for the entry date I use the midpoint of a candidate's first disclosure report; as an approximation for the funding date I use the midpoint of the period in which the campaign received the amount. These values are doubtless subject to some measurement error, but there is no reason to think the error covaries with reported self-financing and fund-raising differently.

"Ain't Nothin' Like the Real Thing"

The effectiveness of an advertising campaign depends in part on the quality of the product being promoted. In early 1985 the Coca-Cola Company spent $34.6 million promoting New Coke (*Los Angeles Times* 1985), but a tidal wave of television commercials could not change the fact that consumers found New Coke unappealing. Within three months, the old taste was back on shelves as Coca-Cola Classic. In a sense, many self-financers are like New Coke—even millions of advertising dollars cannot make them attractive to voters. This suggests an interaction between funding and quality—funding may be effective in proportion to the fundamental appeal of the candidate. Political consultant Garry South invoked this theory explaining Al Checchi's defeat in California's 1998 Democratic primary for governor. South, the campaign manager for then lieutenant governor Gray Davis, recounted,

> I said it's the old story about the cat food company. The president calls in all the sales people and is reading them the riot act because sales are way down. He says, "You know, we've got the best designed can, and we've got the best advertising agency in America doing this, and we've got great ads on the air and everything else. Why can't we sell any cat food?" And after a moment of silence, one of the salesmen raises his hand and says, "Because, sir, cats don't like it." Now, you can't sell a candidacy if the cats don't like it. And from July of '97 forward, that is what I saw here. [Checchi] was easily croakable. (Lubenow 1999, 100)[9]

This idea is not without precedent in the political science literature (as Garry South undoubtedly knew). Green and Krasno found that "challenger spending is more productive in the service of a high-quality challenger" (1988, 893–94). In fact, Green and Krasno's results suggest that spending is *only* effective in combination with quality—the coefficient of an interaction term for spending and quality is significant, while the coefficient of spending alone is not (table 4, 893; table 6, 899).

An interaction effect is a theoretically sound explanation for the gap

---

9. Five years later self-financing was much more productive against Davis, as the popular film star Arnold Schwarzenegger replaced Davis as governor in an unusual recall election, spending $8 million of his own money.

between self-financing and fund-raising; however, empirically it does not appear to explain the gap at all. The gap persists *when candidate elective experience is held constant,* so variation in candidate quality within any single group is minimized. If quality variations of this magnitude significantly influenced the effect of funding, one would expect elective experience, an excellent indicator of candidate quality, to have a very strong impact on funding's productivity. Under the "cat food" theory, experienced candidates should get significantly more mileage out of funding than inexperienced candidates. In these data it is not clear that they do. Self-financing appears more effective for experienced candidates than inexperienced candidates, but the differences are not statistically significant for either challengers or open-seat candidates. Among challengers, contributions are more productive for inexperienced candidates than experienced candidates, and among open-seat candidates, there is virtually no difference. If there is an interaction effect, it is quite small; otherwise there would have been clearer, consistent differences between experienced candidates and inexperienced candidates with respect to the effect of campaign contributions.

It is possible, however, that elective experience is more like the design of the ads than the taste of the cat food. Although elective experience is an excellent measure of candidates' skills, name identification, and reservoir of committed supporters, perhaps it is not a very good measure of candidates' fundamental appeal to voters. Appeal may have much more to do with personality than politics. To put it plainly, it is possible that there are just as many jerks in the population of experienced candidates as there are in the population of inexperienced candidates, and jerkiness may correlate with self-financing. But if appeal is a key variable for getting elected, candidates who have succeeded in getting elected to some lower office probably have at least some appeal. It thus seems unlikely that an interaction with candidate quality is to blame for the difference between self-financing and fund-raising.

How Money Is Spent

Chapter 5 will take up the issue of how campaign funds are spent, and we will see that self-financing does seem to impact how candidates allocate their campaign budgets. Self-financers tend to spend more money on "one-way campaigning" (advertising) and less money on two-way campaigning (interaction with voters). It is beyond the scope of this book to investigate what kinds of expenditures are more or less productive, but the fact that differences across candidates relate to self-financing suggests an explanation for the productivity gap between self-financing and fund-raising. Perhaps self-financers simply don't know how to run a campaign and waste their money on fruitless expenditures.

There is some anecdotal evidence that this is the case. Sara Fritz, a journalist who has written extensively about campaign finance issues, offers the following analysis.

> The first mistake [rich candidates] typically make is to hire too many high-priced consultants....Another common mistake of self-financed candidates is they spend too much money on unnecessary or frivolous things. Records showed [Steve] Forbes paid one of his consultants $223,000 in one month, [Al] Checchi continued to make high-priced media buys long after it was apparent he was going to lose, and Corzine's spending has included at least $11,000 for chauffeurs. (2000)

Senator Robert Bennett (R-Utah), himself a onetime extreme self-financer, provides another illustration in describing his 1998 race.

> I found that spending $6.2 million in Utah in a primary can become a self-defeating kind of activity. He ran out of places to spend it. He was buying ads on the Saturday morning cartoons because there weren't any other places to buy ads. That caused him, frankly, some problems, as people laughed a little bit at that. (U.S. Senate 2001a)

House self-financers are also known to squander their money. Regarding a politically inexperienced businessman who lost a 2000 Republican primary in California's Silicon Valley, one Bay Area columnist quipped, "His name may have been Bill Peacock, but it appears campaign consultants plucked him like a prize turkey" (Simon 2000).

How Money Is Collected:
The Process of Fund-Raising vs. the Act of Self-Financing

Congressman Tom Davis characterized the extreme self-financer as "the individual who can go to McDonald's, have breakfast with himself, write himself a $3 million check, and have the largest fund-raising breakfast in history" (U.S. House 2002b). As Davis's portrait suggests, all campaign dollars are not created equal. Consider the qualitative difference between writing oneself a check for $3 million over an Egg McMuffin versus raising $1,000 from each of 3,000 voters. In both cases the campaign adds $3 million to its bank account, but only in the latter situation does it also add—or at the very least solidify—support from 3,000 individuals, adding to the bank of political capital. In a 2004 House primary one candidate said of his rival, "He doesn't have any support" despite the rival's (mostly self-financed) million-dollar campaign treasury (Helm 2004).

Indeed, the value of raised campaign receipts entails much more than purchasing power. Contributions can serve to signal a candidate's strength to other players—potential opponents, opinion leaders, reporters, strategic campaign contributors. As Herrnson notes, "Symbolically, [small contributions] are often viewed as an indicator of grass-roots support" (1995, 131). Self-financing, on the other hand, indicates the support of a single individual—the candidate himself. Similar amounts of contributions and self-investment may represent similar levels of *financial* viability, but only contributions signal *political* viability. All else being equal, a candidate who self-finances $100,000 can purchase the same quantity of campaign services as a candidate who raises $1,000 each from 100 constituents, but the fund-raiser starts off 100 votes ahead of the self-financer. If the fund-raising candidate solicits contributions from groups his political support may be even broader, as a single group can represent dozens to thousands of individual members.

Individual contributions are more than an indicator of grassroots support; they may often also be a cause of support. In other words, political support may be built or strengthened by fund-raising activity. Herrnson comments, "[Fund-raising events] are also helpful in generating favorable press coverage and building goodwill among voters" (1995, 135). Herrnson referred specifically to events, but most fund-raising is the product of individual solicitations (Steen 1999). Even these individual contacts add value to a campaign. Consider the mechanics of "dialing for dollars," as fund-raising is called by its practitioners: a candidate contacts an individual or the leader of a local group and personally requests that person's or organization's financial support. The bid for political support is usually implicit (although sometimes explicit), and indeed a financial contribution is often the precursor of a public endorsement or a commitment of manpower. For example, most federal candidates in the Democratic Party are familiar with the process of raising money from labor unions. The candidate must first make her pitch to the local affiliates in her area. The locals then submit a request to their national unions. The national organizations cut checks in varying amounts, the local unions then supply their members to staff phone banks, walk precincts, put up yard signs, and otherwise assist with the grassroots or field campaign. In other words, contributions in any amount and from many kinds of sources add both financial and political value to a campaign. The fringe benefits of fund-raising—that is to say, voter contact and publicity—do not accrue to candidates who write the checks themselves.

SUMMARY

The advantage of personal wealth is by no means insurmountable. In one sense the advantage is certainly unfair since it is not universally available to candidates. But as described earlier, self-financing has not actually propelled hordes of rich candidates into the House of Representatives. Rather, the effect of personal funds on vote margins and election outcomes is quite small. We saw that $1 million in personal funds only buys 5 to 10 points on Election Day. Since contributions add political value to campaigns that self-financing does not, self-financers' opponents do not have to match them dollar-for-dollar in order to stay competitive. In fact, self-financers tend to be inexperienced, low-quality candidates, so in many cases their personal funds do little more than make them more competitive with their stronger opponents. This is especially true of challengers.

The results of this empirical analysis will likely surprise many, especially those who believe that money dictates election outcomes and that the burgeoning amount of personal funds in congressional elections spells danger for democracy. Yes, some self-financers swamp their opponents financially but they do not always—or even usually—bury their opponents at the ballot box. Self-financing does give some candidates an edge but only in comparison to how they would have fared without spending personal funds. In most cases, even extreme self-financing has little effect on who stands in the winner's circle.

CHAPTER 5

Self-Financing and the Electoral Connection

THE FOCUS OF THIS BOOK is the process of elections, but let us not overlook the fact that elections are primarily significant as instruments, not ends. The menu of alternatives, level of competition, and tally of the votes are all important because they determine who serves in public office and, to some extent, how. It is thus appropriate to conclude with a discussion of self-financing in the context of the "electoral connection" to representation, to use David Mayhew's term.

There are three ways in which self-financing can telegraph from the electoral context to governing. First, elections are the selection mechanisms that determine which candidates serve as representatives and, consequently, the personal characteristics and qualifications of officeholders. When more self-financers win, more self-financers hold office. What, then, are the qualities that distinguish self-financers? Second, elections provide incentives to candidates to ingratiate themselves with those who can help them get elected. Self-financing can ease the pressure to take positions that please campaign contributors, but does it? Third, the experience of campaigning shapes candidates' perspectives on their constituencies and on the political process. As Richard Fenno notes, "A [congressman] cannot represent any people unless he knows, or makes an effort to know, who they are, what they think, and what they want; and it is by campaigning for electoral support among them that he finds out such things" (1978, 233). Are there any patterns to self-financed campaigns that affect how a candidate perceives his constituents? This chapter addresses these three questions by focusing on the 315 potentially competitive nonincumbents who first won seats in Congress from 1992 through 2000.

CHARACTERISTICS OF SELF-FINANCED REPRESENTATIVES

Hannah Pitkin (1967) distinguishes between two major kinds of representation, "standing for" something and "acting for" something. Political scientists have since come to label these two categories *descriptive representation* and *substantive representation*. *Descriptive representation* refers to the correspondence between the outward characteristics of a representative and those of the represented. "In political terms," Pitkin writes, "what seems important is less what the legislature does than how it is composed" (61). A familiar articulation of the principle of descriptive representation is Bill Clinton's 1992 campaign promise, "I'll give you an administration that looks like America" (Black 1992).

Descriptive representation has been invoked in the debate over self-financing. The problem with overrepresentation of self-financers is that it implies overrepresentation of the rich. Tellingly, one critic of self-financing decried "a government of millionaires" (Sher, LaPolt, and Woods 1996, B1), not "a government of people who loaned money to their own campaigns," while another warned of "plutocracy" (Buckley 2000), and a third lamented that "the political system [is in] the clutches of wealthy candidates" (*New York Times* 1996). These comments do not attack self-financing qua self-financing; rather they attack self-financing as a vehicle for favoring rich candidates. Candidate self-financing seems to undermine the principle of descriptive representation, or the correspondence between characteristics of the governors and characteristics of the governed.

Indeed, self-financing is very strongly correlated with measures of personal wealth. Among new members of Congress elected from potentially competitive districts, the correlation between self-financing and the value of House candidates' assets is .15 ($p < .01$). When two extreme outliers are omitted the correlation balloons to .54 ($p < .001$).[1] The correlation is also strong among general election losers ($r = .39, p < .001$) and primary election losers ($r = .20, p < .001$).

---

1. The outliers are Michael Huffington, who self-financed three times as much as any other successful nonincumbent, and Jane Harman, whose personal wealth in 2000 was more than twice as large as any other successful nonincumbent. Harman self-financed $823,000 in her first bid for Congress in 1992, then in 2000 when she sought to reclaim the seat she had vacated two years earlier she did not self-finance at all. The value of candidates' personal assets is calculated from candidates' Personal Financial Disclosure statements. Please see appendix A for a description of the measurement strategy for this and other wealth-related variables.

TABLE 5.1.   Mean and Median Value of Candidate Assets and Income, by
Self-Financing Level: New House Members from Potentially Competitive Districts

	Mean Value of Candidate Assets ($)	Median Value of Candidate Assets ($)	Mean Value of Income ($)	Median Value of Income ($)	N
Non-self-financers	927,812	101,003	106,834	85,197	70
Minimal self- financers	296,925	115,531	93,244	78,172	128
Moderate self-financers	1,456,613	696,522	232,846	107,181	44
Extreme self-financers	3,050,169	1,343,017	382,798	157,928	14

That self-financing is positively correlated with candidate wealth suggests that personal spending does indeed exacerbate the overrepresentation in Congress of the well-to-do. However, a correlation coefficient does
not reveal anything about the magnitude of differences among candidates.
Self-financing could be perfectly correlated with wealth and still have little consequence for descriptive representation if, say, differences between
extreme self-financers and non–self-financers were substantively small. But
they are not. As table 5.1 demonstrates, the mean wealth of extreme self-
financers in House elections ($3 million) is about three times the average
wealth of non–self-financers ($927,812). The disparity in median wealth
is even larger, as the median among extreme self-financers ($1.3 million)
is thirteen times the median among non–self-financers ($101,003).

One should not overlook the fact that even non–self-financers are considerably better off than the population at large. Consider, for example,
the variable *annual income,* the amount of salary and investment income
House candidates reported in the calendar year preceding the election.
Income can be measured somewhat more precisely than assets and can
also be compared more readily to national income statistics. Average candidate income was $106,834 for non–self-financers, $93,244 for minimal
self-financers, $232,846 for moderate self-financers, and $382,798 for
extreme self-financers. The median income for American households in
1990 was $28,951 (CensusCD 1996), a fraction of the typical income of
congressional candidates.[2] Adding self-financers to the membership does

2. Interestingly, the income gap between Americans and their elected representatives
likely grows slightly once those representatives take office. The average *salary* reported by
nonincumbent winners in the year prior to their election was $85,486, less than the start-
ing congressional salary of $133,600 in effect in 1993, the first year in which these can-
didates began to serve in the U.S. House of Representatives.

contribute to the overrepresentation of the wealthy in Congress, but without self-financers Congress would certainly not be a perfectly accurate reflection of the population.

Extreme self-financers may not be descriptively representative of the American population, but some of them may not be such bad matches to the populations in their own congressional districts. Indeed, three of the largest House self-financers, Ellen Tauscher ($1.7 million in 1996), Jane Harman ($823,000 in 1992), and Brad Sherman ($589,299 in 1996), happen to represent affluent districts in which median household income is about $50,000. There are significant numbers of wealthy constituents in California's Contra Costa County, Palos Verdes Peninsula, and San Fernando Valley, the areas represented by Tauscher, Harman, and Sherman, who are descriptively represented by their rich congresswomen and -man. However, despite these three examples there is no general tendency for self-financers to come from wealthy districts. In fact, there is a slightly positive correlation between candidate income and district income, but it is not statistically significant. Perhaps one could say the good news is that the relationship between candidate income and median district income is not negative. Rich candidates are not concentrated in poor districts, where they would be most unlike their constituents. But candidate income nearly always exceeds median constituent income by quite a lot. Obviously, the mismatch between candidates and their districts is more pronounced when candidates have self-financed more. Table 5.2 reports the average difference between a candidate's income and her constituency's by level of total self-financing. For successful non–self-financers, the average difference between candidate income and constituency income was $74,001; the difference climbs to $349,005 for extreme self-financers.

TABLE 5.2. Mean Difference between Candidate Income and Median Household Income in District, by Self-Financing Level: New House Members from Potentially Competitive Districts

	Mean Difference ($)	N
Non-self-financers	74,001	70
Minimal self-financers	62,040	128
Moderate self-financers	201,889	44
Extreme self-financers	349,005	14
All candidates	105,040	256

An alternative (and sometimes complement) to descriptive representation is *substantive representation,* which refers to the actual activity of representatives: what they do, how they behave, the issues they pursue. Some self-financed candidates counter that personal financing enhances substantive representation, claiming that financial independence allows them to pursue their constituents' interests without having to consider the wishes of campaign contributors. Charles Owen, a candidate for Kentucky's Democratic U.S. Senate nomination in 1998, noted that because he relied on personal funds to run his campaign, "I won't owe the special interests anything" (Cross 1998). Owen implied that he would be a better representative for Kentuckians than a senator who would feel pressure to repay his contributors, including the "special interests" among them, for their financial support. Similarly, a campaign spokesman for Cliff Oxford, a Democratic Senate candidate in Georgia whose personal spending triggered the BCRA Millionaires' Amendment in 2004, argued that self-financing would make Oxford "an independent voice in the Senate, not controlled by special interests" (Kurtz 2004).

As David Mayhew notes, "What a congressman has to try to do is to insure that in primary and general elections the resource balance (with all other deployed resources finally translated into votes) favors himself rather than somebody else" (1974, 43). This is equally true of the *aspiring* congressman. Incumbents, challengers, and open-seat candidates alike keep the resource balance favoring themselves by taking positions that will appeal to a majority of the electorate in their jurisdictions. To communicate that they have done so requires expenditures, as even the most accomplished publicity hound needs funds to advertise himself to the voters. It has been said that "the most dangerous place in Washington [is] the space between Chuck Schumer and a television camera" (Harpaz 1998, 1A), but Schumer, widely regarded as an expert at attracting media coverage, still raised $16.7 million for his 1998 campaign against incumbent Republican senator Alfonse D'Amato. Without campaign funds, whether from the candidate or contributors, there can be no paid staff, no booth at the county fair, no bumper stickers or buttons, and certainly no television ads or mailed brochures. Having saved Medicare, stopped drug trafficking, or created 100,000 new jobs does not help a candidate much if the voters do not know about it. In campaigns, the tree falling in the forest certainly does *not* make a sound if it is not recorded for a thirty-second ad.

Because they must both take positions and advertise them, candidates have incentives to satisfy two groups, potential voters and potential contributors. These groups are not mutually exclusive but they are distinguishable. Potential voters include all citizens over the age of seventeen who reside within the election district. In primary elections the universe of potential voters is additionally limited (in most states) by the requirement that they belong to the political party in whose primary they seek to participate. Many, but not all, of these individuals have the capacity to contribute campaign funds, but the universe of potential contributors also includes all citizens residing outside the election district and, in the case of federal elections, registered political action committees, which may be based anywhere in the United States but are usually headquartered in Washington, D.C.

Neither constituents nor contributors are uniform in their preferences within their respective groups, but let us consider what happens when a particularly generous contributor conflicts with an important group in the constituency on a particular policy or set of policies. A candidate must decide whether to side with the constituency or the contributor. The candidate must determine how much heeding the constituent group will cost him in lost campaign contributions and compare the number of votes gained (or preserved) from the constituency to the number of votes he could attract with the contributors' financial support. The popular perception (although perhaps not the reality) is that most candidates choose to satisfy the contributor most of the time.

Self-financing one's campaign can eliminate the need for this choice. If one does not need financial support from contributors he can always side with the constituency, and many self-financers have touted their freedom to do so. Jon Corzine and Herb Kohl even invoked this principle in their campaign slogans, running as "Unbought and Unbossed" and "Nobody's Senator But Yours," respectively. (Many self-financers later borrowed the phrase first used by Kohl.) The underlying idea appeals to some voters. Speaking to a reporter about Corzine's huge personal outlays, one New Jersey longshoreman echoed the campaign spin: "No one can tell him what to do. If he wins, they can't hold nothing over his head" (Jacobs 2000). However, political pollsters have not found any consistent patterns with respect to voters' evaluations of the merits of self-financing

(Associated Press 2000; Halbfinger and Connelly 2000; Public Policy Institute of California 1998).[3]

The implicit argument put forth by Corzine, Kohl, and others is that candidates who self-finance are better representatives than candidates who raise money. Campaign contributions are depicted as corrupting, giving the "special interests" an advantage over the public, while self-financing purportedly renders candidates "independent" and allows them to pursue the public good. Yet when one sifts through the rhetoric to consider the underlying incentives for both fund-raisers and self-financers, the contrast is not as stark as the sound bites suggest. Rather, the comparison overstates both the corrupting power of campaign contributions and the purity of self-financing.

Overstating the Corrupting Influence of Contributions

It is commonly assumed that (1) contributors and voters have conflicting interests, and (2) the recipient of a contribution resolves that conflict in favor of the contributor (see Smith 1995, 91, for a catalog of works arguing that campaign contributions result in "the overrepresentation of special interests in Congress"). But as Smith notes, "the evidence that is presented by journalists and others in support of this argument is seriously flawed" (1995, 91). In fact, the conflict between contributors and voters is often exaggerated, and there is no compelling empirical evidence that contributors' interests actually do prevail over constituents'. In a comprehensive review of the literature on interest group influence, Smith concludes that "the findings are both conflicting and suspect, and thus ultimately inconclusive" (1995, 123). Smith cites several studies that find no impact of contributions on roll call votes (92). The articles that do identify a relationship do not pin down the direction of the causal arrow (92). That is to say, they are unable to determine whether congressmen take a position because they received campaign contributions, or whether donors make campaign contributions because a congressman took their position.

---

3. As mentioned in chapter 1, several political consultants have personally told me that their polling turned up no evidence that voters either punish or reward self-financers for campaigning with personal money. The results of these polls are the proprietary information of the clients for whom they were conducted and thus cannot be officially cited or identified.

To date neither journalists nor scholars have satisfactorily demonstrated that the correlation between roll call votes and campaign contributions is not explained by representatives' a priori issue positions.

Special interests and constituency interests.   There is also a tendency to vilify contributors, especially organized contributors, as "special interests" and to exaggerate the dissimilarity between the "special interests" and constituency interests. In fact, many of the so-called special interests represent segments of individual electoral constituencies. One might disparagingly call the AFL-CIO "Big Labor" but it is in fact a federation of unions comprised of individual workers. The National Rifle Association, also known as "the gun lobby," is a group of dues-paying gun owners and Second Amendment rights advocates. The much maligned trial lawyers? They're people too, individual members of the bar who represent plaintiffs in court. The teachers' unions, the Sierra Club, the U.S. Chamber of Commerce, and the National Right-to-Life Committee are all voluntary associations whose members are individually somebody's constituents, and it is entirely legitimate for them to seek representation whether or not they make organizational campaign contributions. Citizens do not forfeit their right to representation when they join formal groups.

The terms *PACs* and *special interests* are often used interchangeably, but in the 1997–98 federal election cycle almost half of all PAC disbursements ($213 million out of $471 million) were made by committees affiliated with labor unions, trade associations, membership groups, or health associations (FEC 1999), all organizations with large individual memberships. The preferences of these PACs are determined by the preferences of group members, many of whom reside in any given contributee's geographic constituency. Even organizational contributors that are not membership groups per se often share interests with significant numbers of real people.

Reform advocates tend to overlook this fact. Consider, for example, *Mother Jones* magazine's 1996 "Dirty Dozen" list of members of Congress. Ranked number 8, Representative Jane Harman (D-California) was, according to *Mother Jones,* "a zealot when it comes to the care and feeding of military contractors" (Pike 1996). The article continues, "Rep. Harman and [other members of the House National Security Committee] . . . benefit from a system in which the billions of taxpayer dollars they direct to military contractors magically transform into the thousands of campaign dollars that help keep them in office." Yet the author himself notes that "Harman's congressional district . . . has the country's largest concentration of defense contractors—including Hughes Electronics, TRW, and Northrop Grumman." In fact, these contractors employed thousands of Harman's constituents. Presumably, assembly-line aerospace workers shared the defense executives' preference for continued government contracts.[4] The 1996 Dirty Dozen also criticized Tom Bliley (R-Virginia), who represented a substantial number of Philip Morris employees, for promoting tobacco interests in Congress, and John Ensign (R-Nevada), who represented thousands of casino workers in Las Vegas, for promoting Nevada gaming interests.

This is not to suggest that because some PAC members are also constituents contributors' interests mirror constituency interests but to point out that these two interests do not always clash, and that often they in fact dovetail. But as noted previously, even when a contributor's interests do conflict with a constituency group's it is unclear whether or how often the contributor tends to prevail. Given the overlap between national organizations and local interests as well as the weakness of empirical research on special-interest influence, the baseline against which self-financers measure themselves is perhaps not as low as one might initially think. Furthermore, the self-financers' position on the scale of purity or independence is somewhat exaggerated.

Overstating the Purity of Personal Financing

The special interest versus public interest contrast ignores a third incentive for representatives: self-interest. Self-financers may simply pursue their own interests instead of those of their would-be contributors. If a congressman can put a campaign contributor's interest ahead of his constituents', as is necessarily implied by those who claim congressmen do put contributor before constituent, why would he not do so when the campaign contributor is himself? A wealthy person with a large stake in a particular company or industry who finds his constituency's interest in conflict with his financial interest has a powerful incentive to put himself first, especially if he wants to self-finance another day. Former New Jersey governor Jim Florio implicitly suggested as much in his 2000 campaign for the Democratic Senate nomination in New Jersey. Florio called

4. In fact, Congresswoman Harman, whom I was serving as campaign manager when the 1996 Dirty Dozen list was published, responded to the article by thanking *Mother Jones* for highlighting her advocacy of the Thirty-sixth Congressional District's economic interests.

his primary opponent Jon Corzine, the former chairman of an investment banking firm, "the senator from Goldman Sachs" (Halbfinger 2000, B1). During floor debate over the Millionaires' Amendment Senator Jeff Sessions (R-Alabama) sounded a similar argument, offering the following observation:

> The Supreme Court, in my view, may not have been perfectly brilliant in the Buckley case in suggesting that an individual who has a lot of money has no potential for corruption. If their money is in one sector of the economy—health care, finance, high tech—if that is where their wealth is and maybe they have another billion dollars of investment, they have a lot to lose. Who says they are more or less corrupt than somebody such as the Senator from Alabama who worked as attorney general and took a State salary every day? I don't know. (U.S. Senate 2001f)

Even if one were to stipulate that a candidate cannot corrupt himself with personal funds, such purity is, in practice, extremely short-lived. Once self-financers get elected most accept campaign contributions as eagerly as any of their colleagues. Virtually no reelection campaigns are financed with personal funds (chap. 1). In the 1992–2000 election cycles, only 57 of 2,062 (2.8 percent) House and Senate incumbents seeking reelection self-financed $50,000 or more.

Consider only potentially competitive candidates who won an election and who sought reelection in the following cycle. Table 5.3 reports the average amount self-financed by each candidate in his initial election and subsequent reelection. In all four categories of self-financing, House candidates radically reduced personal funding in their first reelection campaigns. Senate self-financers actually increased personal spending in their first reelection campaigns, although the average difference is not statistically significant. However, Senate candidates also increased their fund-raising markedly in their first reelection bids, as did House candidates. This is especially true for candidates who self-financed heavily in their initial campaigns, and it seriously undermines the assumption that self-financers are incorruptible by virtue of their reliance on personal funds. The differences between fund-raising in the first and second campaigns are statistically significant for both House and Senate candidates.

The presumption of self-financers' independence is further undermined by self-financers' reliance on personal loans to fund their campaigns. There

TABLE 5.3. Average Self-Financing and Contributions in First Election and First Reelection, by Chamber: Potentially Competitive New Members Who Sought Reelection

	Senate		House	
	First Election	First Reelection	First Election	First Reelection
Self-Financing				
Non-self-financers	$ 0	$ 11	$ 0	$ 663
N	9	9	83	83
Minimal self-financers	$ 3,911	$ 43,300	$ 14,556	$ 2,983
N	5	5	157	157
Moderate self-financers	$ 164,868	$ 425,171	$105,728	$ 8,631
N	6	6	66	66
Extreme self-financers	$2,265,000	$2,538,029	$671,485	$ 31,312
N	1	1	13	13
All candidates	$ 155,894	$ 252,650	$ 56,403	$ 4,702
Total N	21	21	319	319
Contributions				
Non-self-financers	$3,507,699	$4,454,588	$579,261	$725,723
N	9	9	83	83
Minimal self-financers	$2,600,300	$6,508,350	$478,996	$686,262
N	5	5	157	157
Moderate self-financers	$3,276,965	$5,385,492	$445,848	$659,070
N	6	6	66	66
Extreme self-financers	$2,704,723	$8,743,586	$456,153	$898,012
N	1	1	13	13
All candidates	$3,187,491	$5,413,790	$497,295	$699,532
Total N	21	21	319	319

is only one substantive difference between self-loans and self-contributions: a self-loan can be repaid, but a self-contribution cannot be refunded to the candidate. The Federal Election Commission has suggested that refunding candidate self-contribution constitutes a "conver[sion of] excess campaign funds to the personal use of the candidate," prohibited under the Federal Election Campaign Act (FEC 1998). The distinction has allowed candidates to use their wealth as political leverage—candidates can spend personal funds to help their campaigns, then later solicit contributions to repay themselves. The only (legal) way to do so is to raise money from campaign contributors, so self-financing with loans sends a strong signal that a candidate intends to repay himself with future receipts.[5]

5. The Millionaires' Amendment to the Bipartisan Campaign Reform Act of 2002 prohibits self-financers from repaying more than $250,000 in campaign self-loans after the

In fact, candidates who self-finance almost always do so with personal loans instead of contributions. From 1992 to 2000, active candidates in potentially competitive elections (other than Jon Corzine) loaned a total of $336 million to their campaigns. They only contributed one-fifth as much, $67 million.[6] Many self-lending candidates who won seats in Congress later raised money from contributors and repaid themselves. The most famous case is Maria Cantwell (D-Washington), who funded her 2000 Senate campaign with bank loans guaranteed by her holdings in Real Networks, the streaming media company where Cantwell became a vice president after leaving the House of Representatives in 1995. Cantwell said in a campaign speech,

> For too long, the powerful special interests have controlled the agenda in our nation's capital, ignoring the people's interest while serving their own narrow interest. That's why I'm spending more of my time talking to the citizens of Washington state than going to Washington, D.C., to solicit campaign contributions. (Postman 2000)

In early 2001 when Cantwell's loans came due the value of her Real Networks stock had plummeted; she scrambled to raise money to avoid defaulting on her loans (Keller and Preston 2001). But one of the most extreme examples of self-repayment is Senator Chuck Hagel (R-Nebraska), who loaned his campaign $1,037,000 in 1996. Hagel repaid himself $787,000 in 1997–98 and $251,625 in 1999–2000, recouping his entire campaign investment (plus $1,625 extra, which seems to be a bookkeeping error).

Table 5.4 summarizes the total amount of self-loans made in initial campaigns, by election year, and the amount of those loans repaid subsequent to the initial election. Over time, members are clearly able to recoup the lion's share of the personal funds they loan to their campaigns. For example, members first elected in 1992 loaned their campaigns a total of $9.9 million during the 1992 cycle, then repaid themselves $6.4 million from 1993 through 2004. Sixty-five percent of all self-loan amounts made

---

date of an election. This new regulation discourages the self-lending form of personal spending (Steen 2005).

6. This figure excludes $13 million in contributions that were actually forgiven self-debt. When a campaign forgives candidate loans the transaction is recorded as both a contribution from the candidate and an equal amount of loan repayment to the candidate.

TABLE 5.4.   Candidate Loans and Subsequent Repayment, by Year: New Members Elected 1992 through 2000

Year of Initial Election	Candidate Loans in First Election ($)	Pre-Election Repayment (through Post-General Report) ($)	Post-election Repayment (Year-End Report through Dec. 31, 2004) ($)	Total Loans Repaid Post-Election (%)	Number of Candidates Making Self-Loans
1992	9,880,189	765,890	6,374,456	65	90
1994	11,336,860	1,014,513	7,098,698	63	76
1996	11,670,017	1,521,510	5,523,934	47	54
1998	24,383,008	3,591,631	1,559,452	6	28
2000	23,808,062	2,282,584	3,373,975	14	23
All new members	81,088,136	9,176,128	23,930,515	30	271

Note: Excludes Jon Corzine; repayments do not include amounts of forgiven self-debt.

in 1992 were subsequently repaid. The class of 1994 also recouped a large percentage of their initial self-loans. Members first elected in 1994 loaned their campaigns a total of $11.3 million in their initial bids and repaid themselves $7.1 million, or 63 percent, from 1995 to 2004. Candidates first elected in 1996, 1998, and 2000 have had less time to chip away at their self-debt, so a larger proportion of their initial self-loans are still outstanding, especially among the class of 1998.[7] Overall, candidates first elected from 1992 through 2000 (excluding Jon Corzine) recouped $23.9 million of $81.1 million loaned, or 30 percent.

It must be noted that the majority of this repayment activity involved candidates who self-financed sparingly or who raised significant amounts from PACs in their first elections. Such candidates would typically not claim independence from the special interests by virtue of self-financing, so their loans and repayments are not of much normative concern here. One should not worry that candidates who self-finance minimally or moderately try to pass themselves off as independent from campaign contributors. Focusing on extreme self-financers only, one finds a smaller (although not insignificant) proportion of self-loans being repaid, especially among senators. Table 5.5 details the self-loan and repayment activity of the twenty-three extreme self-financers who won seats in Congress. Together they loaned a total of $51.3 million to their initial campaigns; by the end of 2004 they had repaid $8.6 million, or 17 percent of total self-

---

7. More than two-thirds of 1998 self-loan amounts were made by a single candidate, Republican Peter Fitzgerald of Illinois. Fitzgerald did not seek reelection in 2004 and forgave his self-loans.

TABLE 5.5.   Candidate Loans in First Election and Subsequent Repayment: Extreme
Self-Financers First Elected to Congress, 1992–2000

Year	Candidate	Candidate Loans in First Election ($)	Repayment of Candidate Loans Subsequent to Election ($)[a]	Percentage of Loans Repaid (%)
Senate				
1994	Bill Frist (R–TN)	3,740,000	2,500,000	67
1996	Chuck Hagel (R–NE)	1,037,000	1,038,625	100+
1996	Gordon Harold Smith (R–OR)	2,603,400	332,110	13
1998	John R. Edwards (D–NC)	6,150,000	0	0
1998	Peter G. Fitzgerald (R–IL)	14,122,500	322,378	2
2000	Maria Cantwell (D–WA)	3,764,625	1,385,819	37
2000	Jon S. Corzine (D–NJ)	60,198,967	0	0
2000	Mark Dayton (D–MN)	8,360,000	134,421	2
	Senate Total[b]	39,777,525	5,713,353	14
House				
1992	Peter Deutsch (D–FL)	358,240	343,240	96
1992	Jane Harman (D–CA)	823,000	0	0
1992	Michael Huffington (R–CA)	0	0	
1992	Herbert C. Klein (D–NJ)	639,000	0	0
1994	Frank A. Cremeans (R–OH)	359,628	99,628	28
1994	John Gregory Ganske (R–IA)	616,177	517,208	93
1996	Christopher B. Cannon (R–UT)	1,496,133	0	0
1996	Merrill A. Cook (R–UT)	0	73,095	
1996	Max A. Sandlin, Jr. (D–TX)	1,157,620	563,450	49
1996	Brad Sherman (D–CA)	672,500	705,100	100+
1996	Ellen O. Tauscher (D–CA)	1,650,000	17,656	1
1998	Douglas A. Ose (R–CA)	1,430,000	0	0
1998	Don Sherwood (R–PA)	739,865	370,852	50
2000	Mike Ferguson (R–NJ)	878,000	0	0
2000	Timothy V. Johnson (R–IL)	720,000	100,512	14
	House Total	11,540,163	2,844,741	25
	House and Senate Total[b]	51,317,688	8,558,094	17

[a]Includes amounts repaid in the year-end reporting period after the election; does not include amounts repaid in the
post-general reporting period; does not include amounts used to retire self-loans; offset by the amount of new loans made
after the initial election.
[b]Jon Corzine excluded from totals.

debt. Extreme self-financers in the House had repaid 25 percent of self-
loans, while Senate self-financers had only recouped 14 percent. Seven of
the 23 extreme self-financers have recovered 49 percent or more of original self-loans, but six have not yet repaid themselves a single dollar (including Jon Corzine, whose $60 million in self-loans is not included in
the total). The richest self-financers are the least likely to recover their
self-loans (fig. 5.1). As candidate wealth increases, the percentage of loans

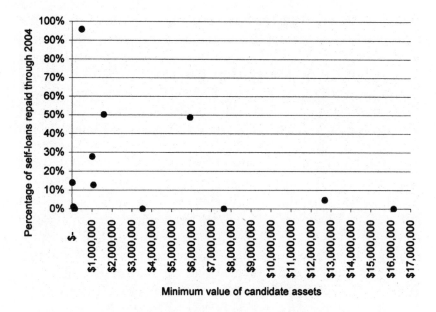

Fig. 5.1.   Percentage of loans subsequently repaid versus minimum value of candidate assets (extreme self-financers elected to Congress, 1992–2000)

recouped clearly decreases. It is also noteworthy that none of the candidates who have repaid the largest percentages of self-loans seem to be on record as claiming political independence by virtue of self-financing.

A wealthy congressman's potential to self-finance in the future may embolden him to oppose his contributors in the present. But incumbents clearly prefer not to self-finance their campaigns, since so few of them do. When one takes a close look at self-financers' activity the basis for their claims of independence start to crumble. The distinction between fund-raisers and self-financers is actually quite fuzzy, since most self-financers demonstrate that they intend to raise contributions, by self-financing with personal loans, then when they win they actually *do* raise money from campaign contributors, either to fund reelection bids or to repay original debt. The contrast is weakened even further by the plain fact that self-financers, like fund-raisers, have strong incentives to keep campaign cash flowing, whether the cash comes from campaign contributors or is self-provided. In the case of self-financers there may be only one contributor, himself, but the self-financer may very well derive more utility from promoting his own interest than the fund-raiser would from satisfying a donor.

Determining whether self-financers are indeed "more independent" than non–self-financed or partially self-financed colleagues is a terribly difficult task. How does one define and measure congressional "independence"? Is a Democrat with a low COPE support score (a rating issued by the AFL-CIO) more independent than one with a high COPE score, or is he just more dependent on antiunion interests? Is a Republican with a low rating from the U.S. Chamber of Commerce more independent than one with a high rating?[8] Locating the baseline or neutral position for each member of Congress is tricky if not impossible.

One can also consider whether self-financers show more independence from their political parties than their colleagues who rely on financial support from the party campaign committees. For example, self-financed senator Peter Fitzgerald (R-Illinois) has been characterized as "a maverick whose independent votes have left him few friends in the party establishment" and as one who has "alienated Republicans in Washington with votes against oil drilling in Alaska, the $15 billion airline bailout and gun control" (Wilgoren 2003). It is somewhat simpler to evaluate members' records of toeing the party line than to judge their loyalty to interest groups. Each year Congressional Quarterly (CQ) identifies roll calls that qualify as party votes, matters on which a majority of one party opposed a majority of the other party. For each member of Congress CQ computes a *party unity score,* the percentage of party votes in which the member voted his party's position. If extreme self-financers are truly free to represent their constituents without pressure from interest groups, they should also be able to buck their parties whenever they please. Such "independent" behavior would manifest itself in lower party support scores.

Table 5.6 summarizes the party support scores in the first year of service for the 323 potentially competitive nonincumbents who won election to the House or Senate. Extreme self-financers, the only candidates to regularly or reasonably claim political independence, are compared to all other candidates combined. Indeed, extreme self-financers do behave differently from their colleagues. The average party unity score for Republican extreme self-financers was 83.0 percent, compared to 88.7 percent

8. One might consider whether the correlation between, for example, individual members' COPE ratings and contributions from labor-affiliated PACs decreases as self-financing increases. However, this effort would be frustrated by extreme self-financers' financial independence. If all campaign funds come from personal fortunes, the correlation between any interest group rating and contributions from that interest group will necessarily be zero.

TABLE 5.6. Mean Congressional Quarterly Party Unity Score in First Year of Congressional Service, by Party and Self-Financing Level: Senators and Representatives Elected 1992–2000

	Republicans	Democrats	All
Extreme self-financers	83.0%	90.4%	85.9%
	14	9	23
Other new members	88.7%	81.4%	85.8%
	179	117	296
All new members	88.3%	82.1%	85.8%
	193	126	319

for other freshman Republicans. In other words, Republican extreme self-financers were less likely than their party colleagues to support the Republican positions in roll calls. The difference is statistically significant and is especially pronounced among House Republicans (table 5.6 does not distinguish between representatives and senators). Among Democrats, extreme self-financers were also significantly different from their classmates, but Democratic extreme self-financers were *more* likely to follow the party's position. The average party unity score for Democratic extreme self-financers was 90.4 percent, compared to 81.4 percent for other Democratic freshmen. (The difference between extreme self-financers and their party colleagues was stronger among senators.)[9]

This inquiry but scratches the surface with respect to self-financers' behavior in office. Still, it offers a preliminary indication that there are notable differences between Democratic and Republican extreme self-financers, a finding especially interesting in light of the party spending patterns identified in chapter 3. The Democratic Party has offered less financial support to extreme self-financers than the Republican Party, but Democratic extreme self-financers have been more loyal to their party on the House and Senate floor than Republicans extreme self-financers. The question of whether extreme self-financers are indeed "independent" remains open, and, given the incentives noted earlier, there is little reason

9. One might wonder if differences in party support scores are an artifact of an idiosyncratic distribution of extreme self-financers across time and party. In some years a party caucus might be particularly unified because of strong party leadership or other factors (consider for example the House Republicans' class of 1994); if self-financers were over- or underrepresented in such a caucus their average party support score would be inflated. However, the pattern evident in table 5.6 persists when party support scores are calibrated to reflect caucuswide variation over time.

to give them the benefit of the doubt. However, the preliminary indication from this analysis of party unity scores suggests that Republican self-financers are indeed more willing than their colleagues to buck party leaders.

Most of a freshman member's knowledge of her constituency has been acquired on the campaign trail. As Fenno notes, "It is, indeed, by such campaigning . . . that a congressman develops a complex and discriminating set of perceptions about his constituents" (1978, 233). The development of those perceptions is shaped by whom the congressman meets and how he meets them.

A candidate who passes her entire day phoning potential contributors is bound to form different impressions than one who spends all of her time shaking hands with the people going in and out of a subway station. Both of these candidates likely see their constituencies quite differently from, say, a candidate who does not bother with personal contact at all and instead relies on poll results to form an ad campaign and a personal check to pay the bills.

By shaping candidates' (and thus representatives') ideas about the people they seek to represent, the nature of the campaign experience has considerable potential to influence the way representatives behave. It is therefore instructive to consider how candidate self-financing is related to the campaign experience. Does the amount a candidate self-finances suggest anything about whom he is likely to meet and under what circumstances the meeting occurs?

Whom Candidates Meet on the Campaign Trail

If political equality is an ideal, which in most forms of democracy (including the American system) it is, citizens should have an equal chance of influencing their elected representatives. One vehicle for such influence is interaction on the campaign trail, so we should want candidates to meet many different kinds of people representing a cross-section of their districts. Political necessity, however, dictates that candidates contact people who are likely to support them, politically and financially, and that this outreach be conducted efficiently.

To raise money candidates have to spend time in the company of individuals who can give it. The more time a candidate devotes to fund-raising, the more his interactions focus on potential contributors, individuals or group representatives who have the means of financial support. Fund-raising is a means of gathering financial and political support but it is also a means of gathering information. Fund-raising affords contributors the opportunity to communicate with their would-be representatives, expressing support for a policy or concern over an issue. So, for example, a candidate who calls through a list of high-tech executives in search of campaign contributions would probably hear a lot about H-1B visas and conclude that they are an important priority. This subject seems unlikely to arise at a PTA meeting or an outdoor arts festival or most other venues in which a candidate would campaign, especially if there are few technology firms in the district.

The more a candidate relies on personal funds, the less attention he needs to devote to potential contributors. But this does not imply that a candidate who is 100 percent self-financed would lend his ear equally to all constituents. Even if candidates had no need for private funding their attention would gravitate to the organized out of the need to attract as many votes as possible in a finite campaign period. A 100 percent self-funded candidate would still have a powerful political incentive to campaign among organized groups. One of Richard Fenno's interview subjects, a congressman, explains, "You go where people meet. That means you spend more time talking to groups like the Chamber than you do to people who live along the road here. . . . The great mass of people you can't reach. They are not organized" (1978, 235).

Since *organized* often connotes *moneyed,* the pure self-financer's universe could look remarkably similar to the fund-raiser's. Even if a self-financer does not need contributions from labor unions he may need the votes of union members. Self-financing may relieve some of the urgency of courting big money, but it does not eliminate the need to focus on organized interests.

The Nature of Campaign Interactions

In *Home Style,* Richard Fenno suggests two possible links between campaigns and representation (1978, chap. 7). First Fenno suggests that congressmen's "home style"—how they behave in their districts—is emblematic of a more general personal style that also manifests itself in Washington. As evidence he cites "Congressman O," one of the 18 members whom

Fenno observed in Washington and on the campaign trail, "who refuses to 'play the groups' at home, [and] also refuses to play them in Washington" (225). Another congressman admits to Fenno that he is equally uncomfortable with what we now call "schmoozing" at cocktail parties whether in his congressional district or the District of Columbia (226). Fenno also notes that members who shy away from firm commitments to their constituencies behave similarly with their congressional colleagues (226–31).

Fenno also suggests a causal link between campaigning and representation. He draws a distinction between one-way and two-way campaigning and argues that each kind of activity has different consequences for the quality of representation. One-way communication is essentially advertising, the candidate's effort to make himself known and liked for the purpose of gaining political support. A candidate engaged solely in one-way communication "cannot know what [his constituents] are like or what they want" because he only transmits, he does not receive information back from the constituency (Fenno 1978, 238). Two-way communication involves interaction between the candidate and constituency and thus entails some degree of responsiveness on the candidate's part. "From the standpoint of democratic theory," Fenno writes, "the greater the proportion of two-way communication, the more likely is there to be both electoral accountability and responsiveness on the part of the representative. Hence, the greater the proportion of two-way communication the better" (1978, 238).

In light of Fenno's observations it is reasonable to consider whether self-financers tend to favor one-way or two-way campaigning any more or less than non-self-financers. A preliminary assessment can be made using information about candidates' expenditures, specifically a data set that lists the amounts spent on twenty-nine types of campaign activity by House nominees in 1994 (a complete description of the categories is provided in appendix F). Spending data give one a sense of the priority candidates assign to different kinds of campaign activity. The amount a candidate spends on things like volunteer expenses may not directly reveal the number of hours he spent campaigning to voters personally, but it does reflect how much attention was devoted to a grassroots effort and is likely related to the candidate's allocation of his own time to various activities.

Six categories of expenditure are especially telling indicators of candidates' reliance on one-way or two-way communication tools: *electronic media, direct mail, other advertising, polling, travel,* and *staff and volunteer expenses.* The first three categories all relate strictly to one-way campaigning, and the amounts spent in these areas are summed to create the variable *one-way campaigning.* The fourth category, *polling,* includes expenditures to learn voters' opinions and so is a form of two-way campaigning. However, polling does not allow constituents to raise concerns themselves; they can only respond to the subjects in the poll questionnaire. Furthermore, much polling centers on testing campaign messages—how does a particular claim play with the voters?—and not on uncovering the fundamental needs and preferences of constituents. Polls do serve as a conduit of information from the public to a candidate, but they do not represent the immersive experience described by Fenno.

The amount spent on travel reflects in part the degree to which a candidate makes personal appearances in his district and is thus a rough indicator of two-way campaigning. (It also of course reflects the size of the district—unsurprisingly, the challenger with the largest travel expenses in 1994 was Cy Jamison of Montana, while several challengers from urban districts reported no travel expenses at all. District size will be held constant in the analysis to follow.) Finally, the category *staff and volunteer expenses* represents traditional grassroots activity typically associated with two-way campaigning, including "all food expenses for staff and volunteers, including phone bank and get-out-the-vote volunteers" as well as "recruitment of volunteers, gifts for staff and volunteers, and staff retreats" (Fritz and Morris 1992, xx). The amounts reported in this category are quite small but they do indicate the extent to which a campaign relied on volunteer efforts, a hallmark of a traditional, personally conducted campaign.

Candidates' allocation of campaign resources is indeed related to how much they self-finance. The more a candidate self-finances, the less he spends on two-way campaign activity and the more he spends on one-way communication. Seemingly unrelated regression illustrates that $100,000 in self-financing corresponds to an additional $13,211 spent on one-way campaigning and $105 less spent on two-way campaigning, when total expenditures are held constant (table 5.7).[10] Self-financing has a positive relationship with spending on polling and a negative relationship with

10. Table 5.7 should not be interpreted as telling a causal story. It tells us how self-financers spend their money without necessarily implying that they spend their money that way *because* they are self-financers.

TABLE 5.7. Seemingly Unrelated Regression: Relationship between Self-Financing and Allocation of Campaign Funds among Challengers in House General Elections, 1994

	One-Way Campaigning Expenditures	Staff and Volunteer Expenses	Polling	Travel
Total self-financing	13,210.9	−105.2	461.8	−439.7
	(4,740.3)★★	(62.1)†	(1,024.4)	(891.3)
Total expenditures	0.5	0.0	0.0	0.0
	(0.0)★★★	(0.0)★	(0.0)★★	(0.0)†
Expenditures squared	0.0	0.0	0.0	0.0
	(0.0)	(0.0)	(0.0)	(0.0)†
Land area of district (in square miles)				3,087.5
				(406.3)★★★
Constant	−13,528.7	−3.4	−339.7	−1,361.8
	(7,570.7)†	(99.1)	(1,636.0)	(1,487.5)
Observations	153	153	153	153

Note: Absolute value of *t*-statistics in parentheses. Appendix F discusses some of the shortcomings of this data and explains why open-seat candidates are not considered.

† $p < .10$ ★ $p < .05$ ★★ $p < .01$ ★★★ $p < .001$

travel-related expenditures (with the geographic size of the district held constant); however, neither of these relationships is large or statistically significant. These relationships hold up in many different variations on the equation estimated so the simplest is presented here.

Our measures of interactive campaigning are by no means perfect, and we only have data for one cycle of candidates. Conclusions about the nature of self-financers' campaign experiences must thus not be stated with confidence. Nonetheless, given these preliminary indicators it appears likely that increased self-financing is associated with decreased constituent contact. One can infer from these patterns that self-financers have less exposure to their constituents than non-self-financers do. How exactly might this affect the way self-financers behave as representatives? The data do not speak to that directly, but at the very least one can speculate that it makes them somewhat less responsive than their non–self-financed colleagues. They have less direct information about their constituents, and their constituents have fewer opportunities to confront them.

DISCUSSION

This evidence suggests that self-financed candidates make different kinds of representatives from candidates who rely primarily on campaign contributions to fund their campaigns. They are descriptively distinct from their colleagues, which is to say they tend to be significantly wealthier, and they engage in different kinds of activity on the campaign trail. These differences do not recommend self-financers as representatives. They are quite unlike the vast majority of citizens, even citizens in more affluent districts. They are less likely than non-self-financers to confront and engage the citizens they seek to represent. Perhaps making up for these shortcomings, they may enjoy greater leeway than most of their colleagues in terms of their relations with and obligations to campaign contributors. However, once elected most self-financers assimilate very rapidly to the norms of fund-raising. Only a small percentage continue to resist the charms of campaign contributors.

CHAPTER 6

Democracy, Campaign Reform, and Politics

IN THE LAST HUNDRED AND FIFTY YEARS, the formal rules of the American political system have been amended to expand the reach of political equality. Yet one of the most fundamental sources of political inequality persists: the unequal distribution of wealth.

The rich man who appears to buy his way into a position of power offends our sense of fairness in the same way that restrictions on the franchise based on property ownership disturb us. It seems an inappropriate transfer of power from the private (economic) sphere to the public (political) sphere. Self-financing candidates have consequently become a popular target of reformers who continue the American crusade to expand equality. All the noise surrounding self-financing candidates assumes that they imperil democracy, but whether they indeed do is a testable—yet until now untested—proposition. This book has presented findings from the first comprehensive investigation of self-financing in American congressional elections. Instead of the overwhelming signs of an electoral system vulnerable to waves of indiscriminate spending, it reveals a set of more subtle effects.

EMPIRICAL FINDINGS

This book has scrutinized several aspects of House and Senate elections, including the conditions under which one should expect candidates to self-finance, the effects of self-financing on other political players, the relationship of self-financing to the balance of electoral communication, the impact of self-financing on election outcomes, and the relationship of self-financing to the electoral incentives and campaign experiences that influence the activities of elected representatives. The pieces fit together to provide an understanding of the full spectrum of electoral consequences when individuals bankroll their own campaigns for Congress.

Chapter 2 illustrated that self-financing is sensitive to the political context, especially in House primaries. Furthermore, candidates strategically allocate their personal investments to take advantage of the yeastlike properties of early money. Extreme self-financers in general elections are an exception; this group alone is prone to last-minute self-financing sprees. These eleventh-hour injections of personal funds likely reflect candidates' efforts to turn the tide in the face of an unpromising election forecast. In other words, self-financing is affected by indicators of the election outcome that are only apparent in the final weeks of a campaign. These indicators, characterized as election-specific idiosyncrasies in chapter 4, likely mask the true relationship between self-financing and election outcomes when it is viewed on its surface.

Chapter 3 probed the relationship between individual candidates' self-financing and the behavior of other political actors. Unlike open-seat status, elective experience, or the other variables analyzed in chapter 2, opposition quality and political party spending can both influence and be influenced by self-financing or anticipation thereof. Strong opposition provides an incentive for—and may even require—candidates to spend their own money on a campaign. At the same time, a self-financed candidacy— or even the threat thereof—can affect the field of other contenders from the self-financed candidate's party. The prospect of facing lavish self-financing spurs some potential candidates to forgo running.

In open-seat contests, every dollar in threatened personal spending reduces the number of expected experienced opponents a self-financer faces in her primary. The chilling effect is especially strong for self-financers with previous experience in elective office. Experienced candidates start off with name identification and a network of past supporters that make them intimidating to opponents; the scare factor is magnified by a capacity to self-finance. However, self-financing by any type of candidate, inexperienced or experienced, open-seat candidate or challenger, does not sway potential opponents from the other major party.

Party leaders' decisions are also shaped by candidates' self-financing. Republican campaign committees appear to reward personal spending at moderate levels by allocating financial aid to candidates who invest in their own campaigns. The Democratic Party takes another tack, spending more money on its non-self-financed and minimally self-financed candidates. While Republicans seem to view moderate personal spending as a sign of viability, Democrats seem to see self-financing as an indicator of financial self-sufficiency.

Chapter 4 began by looking at direct measures of candidates' ability to overwhelm their opposition with resources drawn from their personal bank accounts. On rare occasions, about 3 percent of potentially competitive primaries and 1 percent of potential competitive general elections, self-financing does open up a wide financial gap between candidates. Personal spending is much more likely to enhance financial parity than undermine it, especially among challengers to incumbent members of Congress. Personal funds are more often used to erase some or all of a financial disadvantage than to swamp an opponent.

The principal finding of chapter 4 was that self-financing is consistently less effective than fund-raising in securing votes. One dollar, a million dollars, or any other amount produces a much larger vote margin if it is raised from contributors than if it is provided by the candidate. This suggests that self-financing is of less value, politically speaking, than fund-raising and is especially true for inexperienced candidates. Among office seekers with no record of officeholding, candidates who self-finance all of their campaign expenditures realize almost no electoral return on their dollars.

This somewhat surprising lesson teaches us that it is not as easy to buy elections as has been suggested in the popular discourse. Indeed, one might conclude that the biggest advantage possessed by self-financers is not their campaign purchasing power but the illusion thereof. The *perception* of strength drives strong opponents away, perhaps providing even more political value than the self-financed expenditures.

Despite the group's political shortcomings some self-financers do get elected, and thus an additional piece of the puzzle concerns the nature of representation provided by self-financed candidates, a topic that warrants extensive study. However, in keeping with the electoral theme of this book, chapter 5 focused on how self-financing relates to electoral conditions, namely, incentives and experiences. Chapter 5 found that, as one would expect, self-financers tend to be wealthier than both Joe Six-Pack and Joe Candidate. Therefore self-financing exacerbates the "unrepresentativeness" of Congress on demographic dimensions. We also learned that House members who self-financed their initial campaigns very rarely self-finance subsequent efforts. In fact, they often repay self-debt from the first campaign by raising money from contributors once they take office. Senators are more likely to be repeat self-financers, but like House members they usually raise significant amounts in their reelection bids. Self-financed candidates' rapid assimilation to the norms of campaign fund-raising undermines their own campaign claims. A mantra of self-financed candidates on the campaign trail is that they are independent from the special interests by virtue of their deep personal pockets; however, these individuals frequently turn to said special interests for contributions, in some instances immediately following their elections. Our one indicator of legislative behavior, members' adherence to a party position in roll call votes, suggests that Republican extreme self-financers are marginally more "independent" than their colleagues, while Democratic extreme self-financers are even more likely than other Democrats to toe the party line.

Finally, the relationship between self-financing and the nature of candidate-constituent interaction was addressed. Obviously, the more a candidate self-finances the less the fund-raising process dominates his perceptions of his constituents. On its face this sounds like a good thing, especially if self-financing allows candidates to devote more time and energy to personal campaigning. However, self-financers tend to eschew more interactive forms of campaigning in favor of one-way forms of communication like television advertising and direct mail. This strategic determination reduces the amount of information self-financers collect *from* their constituents and makes one wonder whether it might be more desirable for them to have some contact with citizens through fund-raising, despite fund-raising's emphasis on affluent citizens. These are preliminary observations in this vein of investigation, but they are suggestive as to the potential pitfalls of a Congress populated by self-financers.

The findings of this analysis are internally consistent. Chapter 3 showed that when strategic actors size up the threat of self-financing they see personal spending by experienced candidates as more potent than personal spending by inexperienced candidates. Chapter 4 confirms the soundness of this judgment, as self-financing by experienced candidates was indeed found to impact vote margins more than self-financing by inexperienced candidates. If self-financing seemed instead to benefit inexperienced candidates more than experienced candidates, we would be left wondering why strategic politicians draw the opposite conclusion. But the same story was told by two distinct variables, opposition quality and vote margins.

This study's good news for democracy is that personal wealth does *not* constitute an overwhelming political advantage. Indeed, the influence of personal spending is considerably more subtle than is implied by the common accusation of self-financers buying elections. Self-financing does improve candidates' vote tallies, albeit modestly and only under certain conditions, and plays a part in shaping the candidate field. In other words, self-financing does buy some votes and a less competitive primary. But the self-financed advantage is typically not large enough to overcome self-financers' own political deficiencies. The wealthy men and women who try to self-finance their way to Washington usually self-destruct en route.

Why does self-financing produce victory for so few candidates? The most important factor undermining self-financers' efforts is their own lack of political experience. Most extreme self-financers are not adequately prepared for a political campaign. In fact, only a small proportion of candidates who rely heavily on personal funding have a background in elective office (chap. 2). It is true that self-financing can neutralize two advantages that experienced politicians enjoy when they run for higher office—name recognition and a base of past contributors. Rich candidates can buy the former and do not need the latter. But money cannot buy a base of past supporters, cultivated in previous campaigns, who have worked for a candidate before and will work for him again. Nor can it buy the campaign skills that many politicians develop on the way up the ladder. As political consultant Darry Sragow puts it, "If you've never lost, or if you've never run before, it's very, very hard . . . to put together the kind of campaign that weathers the kind of storms that you face [on the campaign trail]" (Lubenow 1999, 128).

Money also cannot buy a record on which to run. Michael Huffington's dad made a bundle in the oil business, and Charles Owen made his money in cable television. But voters in California and Kentucky didn't seem to think these credentials qualified either man for a Senate seat. In contrast, successful self-financers have touted experience in public life, if not in public office. Garry South, a campaign consultant in California, illustrates the point by contrasting a successful self-financer to an unsuccessful one.

> Dick Riordan . . . had 30 years of grassroots, hard core experience in the community, setting up foundations, putting computers in housing projects. And [Al] Checchi comes along having no record . . . of any kind of deep, long community involvement that counterbalanced the fact that he was just some fly-by-night rich guy. (Lubenow 1999, 128)

Riordan was elected mayor of Los Angeles in 1993, while Checchi lost a bid for California governor in the 1998 Democratic primary.[1] Another veteran of self-financed campaigns, media consultant David Doak, echoed that "rich guys can win ... [if] they're decent human beings with a record of contribution to their community" (Lubenow 1999, 128–29).

Perhaps because of their inexperience, self-financers tend to wage strategically imbalanced campaigns. They often fail to provide strong ground support for the air war. That is, they often rely heavily upon television advertising without carrying out a field campaign that has multiple benefits. Personal campaigning allows the candidate to connect with voters, to link into networks of political activists, and to overcome the image of a wealthy dilettante that seems to plague self-financers. Self-financers do not know from firsthand experience the value of interaction with voters and thus generally do not devote time and energy to activities that will fulfill this part of an effective electoral strategy. Those wealthy candidates who deviate from this pattern—examples include U.S. senator Jon Corzine (D–New Jersey) and attorney general Eliot Spitzer (D–New York)— have met with more success on the campaign trail.

SELF-FINANCING AND DEMOCRATIC PRINCIPLES

The most precise calculation of coefficients yields little insight into the implications of self-financing for students of American democracy. Rather it is the interpretation of the quantitative data that provides both understanding of the operation of our political institutions and lessons for those who would attempt to improve them. What then are the implications of this book's empirical findings for political equality and electoral competition, the principles at the heart of the American democracy?

Political Equality

As noted at the outset of this chapter, the concept of political equality has evolved considerably since the Founding. The Framers were largely un-

---

1. Ironically, Riordan was the experienced politician running against a self-financing novice in the 2002 Republican primary for California governor. William Simon Jr., who was typically described in news accounts as a "millionaire" and the son of a former treasury secretary, received 49 percent of the GOP primary vote to Riordan's 31 percent.

troubled by the conflation of economic inequality and political inequality (e.g., Beard [1957] 1987). Expansions of the franchise have provided formal political equality to increasingly large proportions of the American public, but the unequal distribution of wealth still compromises de facto political equality. If political expression were costless, economic inequities would not result in political equality, at least not as much as they do now. But campaigns cost money, so people who *have* money enjoy an advantage over people who have to *get* money. This reality indicates prima facie inequality in the system. Is the surface inequality accompanied by material inequality?

The empirical analysis suggests that the advantage of personal wealth is by no means insurmountable, as a self-financer's opponent's qualities can negate that advantage. For example, if a self-financer's general-election opponent raises $550,000 (the average amount raised by opponents of inexperienced open-seat candidates), the self-financer's predicted margin decreases by up to about 5 points.

Judging the extent to which self-financing undermines political equality in primary elections is more difficult. We do not have direct evidence of the effect of self-financing on primary candidates' votes, but it is reasonable to infer that self-financing helps primary candidates more than party nominees. There are two pieces of circumstantial evidence to support this conclusion. First, Gary Jacobson's (1975) study of broadcast spending suggests that the things money can buy influence primary election results more than general election results. Second, the analysis of the deterrent effect suggests that self-financing is "scarier" in primaries than in general elections. (Strategic politicians were correct to judge self-financing by experienced candidates "scarier" than self-financing by inexperienced candidates, and they may be right about the difference between primary and general-election self-financing, too.) But if campaigns matter more in primaries than in general elections then self-financers' lack of experience may undermine their own efforts. Self-financing may constitute a bigger advantage in primaries, but self-financers' weaknesses also constitute a bigger disadvantage.

Ideally the political system would put all candidates on equal footing. The ability of one candidate to spend exorbitant, or even modest, sums of money on his or her own campaign is inherently unfair, to be sure. But one's concern over this inequality should be tempered somewhat by the empirical evidence that the self-financer's advantage, while unfair, is not always (or usually) insurmountable.

Electoral Competition

Robert Dahl argues that two essential conditions for the political form he labels "polyarchal democracy" are an unbounded set of alternatives and a uniform distribution of information about each alternative across the population (1956, 69–70).[2] The concern that self-financers can "buy elections" is in part motivated by concerns that these two conditions are not met. In other words, "buying an election" is not only unfair to the losing candidate, it is unfair to the voters who are deprived of a meaningful choice among vigorously competing alternatives.

Dahl notes that it is difficult to measure a political system's conformance to these two conditions (1956, 86). However, the task is made much easier when one focuses on a discrete piece of the system as in this study. Indeed, the variables *experienced opponents,* indicating the number of choices, and *funding ratio,* indicating the likelihood of information being evenly distributed, are naturally measured on an ordinal scale. One can therefore judge how self-financing affects these aspects of electoral competition and comment on their implications for democracy.

Self-financing deters experienced opposition from competing for elective office and thereby reduces the number of alternatives available to the voters. On its face, this finding appears to signal deterioration, not improvement, in democratic conditions. Moreover, self-financing contributes to severe financial imbalances between opposing candidates in some situations. This too is hardly ideal. But there are mitigating circumstances that should be considered before we declare self-financing the bane of vigorous competition.

The number of candidates actually deterred by self-financing is not large. In fact, if one sums up the number of *deterred* opponents predicted for each individual candidate, the statistical analysis suggests that anticipated self-financing reduced the number of experienced candidates running in potentially competitive House primaries by a total of 92. The observed number of experienced candidates in those primaries was 334, so one can infer that self-financing reduced the total number of experienced alternatives by about 21 percent. Of course, in some individual contests self-financing had a much larger effect than in others. There were 54 candidates

---

2. These are Dahl's fourth and fifth conditions, respectively. Dahl does not overlook the importance of political equality, as his second condition for polyarchal democracy is that "the weight assigned to the choice of each individual is identical" (1956, 67).

for whom the predicted effect of *anticipated primary self-financing* was to reduce the number of experienced opponents by half or more. Still, these candidates constituted less than 4 percent of the sample. In substantive terms, the deterrent effect cannot be said to represent a serious threat to the quality of electoral competition in House elections generally.

Self-financing may reduce the number of experienced choices, but by allowing inexperienced candidates to campaign more effectively it can also be seen as adding to the menu of alternatives. This may seem no consolation to those who feel that experience in lower office is an important qualification for congressional service. But to those who believe that the Congress is dominated by career politicians and could benefit from more diversity in the professional and political backgrounds of its members, the addition of a self-financed candidate to the slate of viable alternatives may be welcome news.

The findings on financial competitiveness also fail to support the notion that self-financing is a widespread, intractable problem for democracy. There is something fundamentally unsettling about an election in which one candidate grossly outspends the others, but this is rarely the case even with extreme self-financers. Instead, self-financing more often allows candidates to even the score, thereby rendering contests *more* competitive than they otherwise would be. And even when self-financing contributes to a gross financial mismatch, we have seen that a political mismatch does not often ensue. In summary, self-financing affects electoral competition in a fashion that we would term antidemocratic, but it does not severely impair the democratic process.

SELF-FINANCING AND CAMPAIGN FINANCE REFORM

Many observers of American politics point to the influence of money in politics as the most important challenge facing our democracy. Such suspicion of money in politics is a long-standing American tradition. As Frank Sorauf notes, "Today's opinion about campaign finance retains the two central premises of the populist and Progressive worldview: a fundamental and implacable distrust of political money, and a disposition to attribute much, even too much, that happens in American politics to it" (1992, 20). As a consequence, extreme self-financing is labeled "obscene" or "offensive" or "disgusting" even when the self-financed campaign crashes and burns. Furthermore, self-financers are accused of buying elections, but in truth their personal expenditures have a fairly small impact on their electoral fortunes. The incorrect impression is undoubtedly reinforced by the few high-profile self-financers who have won. Most recently, Michael Bloomberg was elected mayor of New York City after spending $78 million of his own money, and of course Jon Corzine, the sixty-million-dollar man, became a senator from New Jersey. But these two politicians are truly exceptional, constituting a group of two that might be called mega-self-financers.

The disconnect between rhetoric and reality has important consequences for both policy and politics. The misperception that the rich can buy seats in Congress distorts campaign finance debate and scares away worthy competitors. The empirical findings of this study offer policymakers a much sounder base from which to construct reform proposals. Significantly, they offer lessons not just about self-financing but also about fund-raising. They also form the basis for evaluation of the Millionaires' Amendment recently adopted by the Congress. Some specific findings and suggestions for how they might guide campaign finance proposals are highlighted next.

The Unappreciated Virtue of Fund-Raising

Fund-raising is often likened to political prostitution, with candidates offering to trade official favors for campaign contributions. Even less extreme views of fund-raising see private campaign financing as a potential vehicle for corruption and for the undue influence of moneyed interests who can afford to play in the campaign finance game. To combat such antidemocratic influences some reform proposals would eliminate fund-raising entirely, replacing campaign contributions with grants from public funds. But public funding may throw the baby out with the bathwater.

The process of amassing financial support is in many ways like garden-variety political campaigning. Candidates solicit support incrementally from individuals and groups who share their positions on one or more issues. When the "support" being solicited is a single vote, this process vitalizes, not undermines, democracy, as the interaction between candidate and constituent makes the candidate a more responsive representative and draws citizens into the political process, thereby enhancing our civil society. But as the emphasis shifts from political support, of which every eligible voter can offer an equal amount, to financial support, which cannot be provided equally by all citizens, the benefits of such interaction are mitigated by the fact that the people involved are not entirely reflective of the political constituency. In other words, the fact that the interaction between candidate and supporter cements a political bond becomes less appealing as the interacting supporters become less representative of the public. But reformers should not overlook the positive aspects of fund-raising entirely. Public financing would reduce opportunities for corruption and the undue influence of contributors that attend privately financed campaigns, but it would also eliminate a powerful incentive for candidates to build relationships with their constituents.

Of course, candidates can and do interact with constituents without asking them for money. A candidate who does not have to raise money (because he receives a public grant with which to pay campaign expenditures) would still be able to campaign personally, and in fact reform advocates often argue that liberating candidates from the demands of fund-raising would increase the amount of time they can spend meeting voters. But there is no guarantee that this would actually happen. In fact, candidates who *do* have reduced fund-raising burdens—because they self-finance their campaigns—do *not* have more personal contact with voters (chap. 5). Rather, they are more likely to rely on impersonal, one-way forms of communication in their campaigns.

Interaction between candidate and contributors is not antidemocratic if the universe of contributors is large and diverse, so perhaps the trick is to give candidates strong incentives to raise from a broad group. A program of public matching funds for small contributions, similar to the system used in presidential primaries, would do so. Such a program could treat in-district and out-of-district contributions differently, reward very small donations much more generously than larger donations, or require support from a minimum number of contributors before a candidate becomes eligible for grants. Matching fund programs can be very narrowly tailored to provide incentives for very specific kinds of campaign behavior.

Note that this proposal is not an antidote to self-financing. The *Buckley* ruling is unambiguous with respect to self-financing, and unless or until it is overturned candidates simply cannot be limited in the amount that they spend on their own behalf.

BCRA and the Millionaires' Amendment

The Bipartisan Campaign Reform Act of 2002 (BCRA) included an amendment intended to reduce the electoral advantage of those wealthy candidates who spend lavishly on their own campaigns. The Millionaires' Amendment attacks the "rich candidate problem" (as *Washington Post* editorial writers once dubbed it) on two fronts, making it easier for self-financers' opponents to raise money and harder for self-financers to recoup their campaign investments after an election. The law establishes trigger amounts of self-financing; if those amounts are exceeded, a self-financer's opponent (or opponents) can raise three or six times the normal limit from individuals, depending on the circumstances. In some cases, self-financing also enables unlimited coordinated expenditures by the opposing party. The Millionaires' Amendment also prohibits self-financers from repaying more than $250,000 in campaign self-loans after the date of an election.

Preliminary analyses of the Millionaires' Amendment suggest that it will have a limited impact on future elections (Steen 2003a, 2006). In 2004 it did deter self-lending to some degree. By restricting the amount of repayments allowed, BCRA essentially made self-financing a riskier tactic. Limits on self-loans also help protect political consumers (i.e., voters) from the bait-and-switch scheme described in chapter 5. Self-financing candidates who claim to be independent of the nefarious special interests are still able to raise money once they are elected, but at least they are sharply limited in how much of that money goes directly into their own pockets. On the other hand, when candidates lent money to their campaigns before BCRA they at least sent a clear signal of their intentions. When a candidate used loans instead of contributions to personally fund a campaign, voters could easily infer that such a candidate intended to raise money from contributors at some point, since the only advantage to loans (over contributions) was the possibility of future repayment. Under the Millionaires' Amendment it is not as easy to predict the future behavior of self-financed candidates. A self-contributor—and all self-financers are essentially self-contributors now—may raise money in the future, or he may not.

Similarly, an analysis of the 2004 congressional elections suggests that increased contribution limits triggered by self-financing had little effect on election outcomes. Of the ninety-three candidates eligible to raise additional funds only one could plausibly credit his victory to the Millionaires'-Amendment fund-raising (Steen 2006). A study of House and Senate elections in the 2000 cycle also indicated that the Millionaires' Amendment would not have affected many races. Of the thirty-five elections in which one candidate's self-financing would have tripped a trigger had

BCRA been in effect, only six could have been swayed by increased fund-raising. However, those six elections included the three most extreme examples of self-financing in the 2000 cycle (the Senate races in Minnesota, New Jersey, and Washington), which are exactly the kinds of races the Millionaires' Amendment was intended to target. In every other election increased fund-raising would not have changed the outcome, either because it would have rolled up a winner's margin or because it would probably not have made up enough ground to overcome a self-financer's overwhelming vote tally (Steen 2003a).

In some ways BCRA seems a step in the wrong direction. Self-financing is commonly used by challengers, and increased contribution amounts will make it easier for some incumbents—who hardly need the help—to defend themselves. This fact is underscored by Senator Chris Dodd (D-Connecticut), who opposed the Millionaires' Amendment to BCRA with these words from the Senate floor.

> We are talking about incumbents who have treasuries of significant amounts and the power of the office which allows us to be in the press every day, if we want. We can send franked mail to our constituents at no cost to us. . . . We do radio and television shows. We can go back to our States with subsidized airfares. . . . I find it somewhat ironic that we are here deeply worried about the capital that can be raised and the candidate who is going to spend a million dollars of his own money to level the playing field. (U.S. Senate 2001d, S2540)

However, only one incumbent actually took advantage of the Millionaires' Amendment in 2004. If that election is typical, the Millionaires' Amendment has done little to undermine challengers.

DIVINING THE FUTURE OF SELF-FINANCING

If politicians learn from their predecessors, self-financing will become both more and less effective in the future. Self-financers themselves will probably learn how to spend their personal funds more wisely, while other strategic actors will realize that they have been overestimating the power of personal spending.

Consider two examples of self-financed candidates who appear to have learned from past mistakes. Eliot Spitzer, who ran for New York state attorney general in both 1994 and 1998, learned from his own personal experience. In 1994 Spitzer self-financed $4 million, placed fourth out of four candidates in the Democratic primary, and received 19 percent of the primary vote. But the experience seemed to teach Spitzer something about what works and what does not, and his 1998 strategy was markedly different. After relying on mass media in his first effort, Spitzer cultivated grass roots—critics might characterize it as purchasing Astroturf—in his second campaign, making personal contributions to Democratic officials and organizations around New York state.[3] In his second campaign Spitzer was able to tout endorsements from a large number of local political figures and deploy activists for a traditional campaign. He also self-financed more than $6 million in direct expenditures, much of which paid for television advertising and direct mail.

Jon Corzine's first campaign for public office was in 2000, when he ran for U.S. Senate as a Democrat in New Jersey. Unlike Spitzer in 1998, Corzine was not a second-time candidate but he made a point of hiring consultants with experience on self-financed campaigns. His media consultant, Bob Shrum, and his polling firm, Penn and Schoen, were both veterans of Al Checchi's failed $35 million effort to become governor of California. Corzine, like Spitzer in 1998, made a strong effort to run a real political campaign and did not rely solely on mass media. He self-financed more than $60 million and won, defeating former governor Jim Florio in the Democratic primary and Congressman Bob Franks in the general election.

Corzine's success and his unconventional strategy (unconventional for a rich candidate, that is) demonstrate that candidates do not have to learn the lesson firsthand, as long as they pay close attention to other candidates. He himself may become a case study for future candidates since his tactics were widely reported in New York and New Jersey media outlets, as well as in political newsletters like *The Hotline*. But this lesson may be lost on a lot of future self-financers if the self-financer personality type centers on the egomaniacal. Self-financers' strategic decisions are not affected by how other candidates from their party have done (chap. 2); this may be because candidates think their own qualities and efforts are paramount. Such self-centeredness could be especially pronounced among wealthy people who are used to individual attention for their accom-

---

3. No one has been able to ascertain the total amount of Spitzer's personal contributions since neither he nor many recipients were required to disclose them.

plishments and, perhaps more important, who do not know any better because they are inexperienced in politics. A description of self-financed Senate candidate Pete Coors (R-Colorado) is a typical assessment of the self-financing personality: "He's the least-suited person I can think of to endure a campaign. . . . he's incredibly private and very thin-skinned" (Johnson 2004, A11).

While the learning curve may make self-financing a more effective means of attracting support, it may also help strategic elites wise up to the reality that self-financing millions of dollars does not by any means guarantee a victory. Consider all the candidates who bowed out of races, only to watch the self-financer they avoided go down in flames. Those candidates might not be so hesitant the next time around, and other experienced officeholders will not want to make the same mistakes. Potential candidates are not the only strategic politicians with something to learn. Party leaders and PAC directors decide how much support to give each candidate, and they will likely be more willing to support self-financers' opponents in the future. Mitch McConnell, the chairman of the National Republican Senatorial Committee in 2000, must have kicked himself for not funding Bob Franks, who came just 3 points shy of defeating Jon Corzine despite being virtually abandoned by his party.

Another factor that may mitigate the increase in self-financing is term limits for state legislators. In the strategic politician's decision calculus, the cost of giving up a current office is what keeps lower officeholders from running for Congress (Jacobson and Kernell 1983). When state legislators are statutorily *required* to give up their seats, they have less to lose by challenging a self-financer. No legislators exhausted their lifetime limit in state legislative service until the 2000 election; as legislators in the fifteen states that now have legislative term limits are kicked out of office, many of them will run for Congress (Steen 2003b). As the pool of strong candidates grows, there will be fewer opportunities for self-financers to win.

The use of personal funds to pay for campaign expenses is a political phenomenon that has been to date little understood yet widely criticized. This study offers the first empirical investigation of the impact of self-financing on the democratic process. I have taken care to consider different aspects of elections and in so doing have revealed interesting, important dynamics. The bottom line is that self-financing has had a surprisingly small effect on election outcomes. Personal funding does buy easier competition and it does buy some votes, but in most cases it does not buy victory.

Appendix A: Variables in the Analysis

Except where otherwise specified, values deemed *self-financing* equal *maximum self-financing* as defined by Clyde Wilcox (1988). *Maximum self-financing* is calculated from data reported in the *byrept* series of spreadsheets distributed by the Federal Election Commission (FEC), which include one record for each individual reporting period and are available at ftp.fec.gov/FEC. Each entry in the *byrept* files discloses the amount of *contributions from the candidate, loans from the candidate,* and *loan repayments to the candidate* in a given report, corresponding to lines 11(d), 13(a), and 19(a) of Form 3, Report of Receipts and Disbursements. I made a great effort to eliminate duplicate entries and identify the correct entry for a reporting period when there were ambiguities in the *byrept* files.

Upon inspecting the actual reports of some candidates I discovered that nonincumbents frequently misreport self-loans in the row for *loans from other sources* (line 13(b), labeled "other loans" in the electronic files).[1] For all candidates in 1994 and 1996 who reported *loans from other sources* in excess of $5,000 I examined Schedule C of Form 3, in which candidates disclose the details of all campaign loans. Where appropriate I recoded certain amounts as *loans from the candidate.* After making these adjustments to the raw FEC data I observed that almost all loans reported by nonincumbents as *loans from other sources* were actually self-loans. I thus recoded all amounts listed in the *other loans* column of *byrept* files as candidate self-loans for nonincumbents in 1992, 1998, and 2000.

---

1. The most common mistake is reporting bank loans that are guaranteed with personal funds or assets as *loans from other sources* instead of *loans personally guaranteed by the candidate.*

Using these amounts I calculated the combined amount of self-contributions and net self-loans (self-loans minus self-repayment) in each reporting period. I then tallied the *cumulative* amounts of self-contributions and net self-loans through the end of each FEC reporting period. Whenever a campaign had *negative* cumulative net loans I attributed the excess repayment to debt retirement from a previous cycle and added the excess repayment back into the net self-loan amount. Often, however, loan repayment is actually loan forgiveness. When a campaign writes off a candidate loan the transaction is recorded as both a contribution from the candidate and loan repayment. Thus whenever I discounted excess loan repayment from maximum self-financing I also discounted candidate contributions, up to the amount of the excess repayment or the amount of candidate contributions, whichever was smaller.

The maximum amount of cumulative combined self-contributions and net self-loans, adjusted as described above, equals *maximum self-financing.* *Maximum self-financing* was tallied for three distinct periods, the primary election, the general election, and the entire two-year cycle. In the text I refer to these distinct measures as *primary-election self-financing, general-election self-financing,* and *total self-financing.*

Contributions equals the sum of amounts reported on lines 11(a)(iii) (Total contributions from individuals), 11(b) (Contributions from Political Party Committees), and 11(c) (Contributions from Other Political Committees) of FEC Form 3. These amounts are also reported in the FEC's electronic data files. In chapter 2 I use the three values separately. As with self-financing, I calculate contributions for three different periods, the primary election, the general election, and the two-year cycle.

Total funding for any given period equals the sum of maximum self-financing and contributions.

Party support is the sum of amounts reported in the FEC *cansum* series of data files in columns labeled party contributions, party coordinated expenditures, and party independent expenditures in favor of the candidate.

For each candidate *funding ratio* is the amount of that candidate's funding, or the sum of *contributions* and *self-financing,* divided by the amount of his opponent's funding. For primary candidates I only computed *funding ratio* for the two candidates who were better funded than all others.

I use *early contributions* as an instrumental variable for *total contributions.* *Early contributions* is the amount of contributions received in the first disclosure filed, as reported in the FEC *byrept* file. Similarly, *early self-financing,* used to create an instrument for *self-financing,* is the amount of contributions and net loans, exclusive of debt retirement from a previous campaign, reported in the first disclosure. *Previous self-financing,* also used for the instrument for *self-financing,* is the amount of maximum self-financing by a candidate in the most recent cycle in which he or she was a candidate. Missing values of *previous self-financing* (for any candidate who did not previously run for office) were set to zero, so whenever *previous self-financing* is used a dummy variable indicating *missing previous self-financing* is also included.

For each candidate, *vote margin* is the percentage of the total vote received by the candidate minus the percentage of the total vote received by his general election opponent. Vote percentages were listed in the FEC *cansum* files. So, for example, in the 1996 general election in California's Tenth District, Democrat Ellen Tauscher received 48 percent of the vote to Republican Bill Baker's 46 percent. Tauscher's *vote margin* was 2, Baker's was −2. The *previous nominee's margin* is simply the *vote margin* for the previous nominee from a candidate's party. Since new district lines were introduced 1992, *previous nominee's margin* is missing for 1992 observations. I set the previous margin to zero in multivariate analysis, which may bias the coefficients of the party/year dummy variables for 1992 slightly.

In a few FEC records a candidate's reported share of the general election vote was incorrect. I corrected those records and can provide SPSS syntax to replicate my changes to anyone who requests it.

If the previous nominee from a candidate's party was unopposed in the general election (i.e., if there was no major-party opponent listed in the FEC data) I set *previous nominee's margin* equal to zero and set a dummy variable, *previous nominee unopposed,* equal to one. If there was no previous nominee, i.e., if the other party was unopposed in the previous election, I set *previous nominee's margin* equal to zero and set a dummy variable, *no previous nominee,* equal to one. This essentially renders the variable *previous nominee's margin* an interaction term, as its coefficient reflects the effect of the margin when the previous election was contested.

Open-seat status is a dummy variable coded one for open-seat candidates and zero for challengers, based on candidate status reported in the column labeled *incumbent/challenger/open seat* in the FEC *cansum* files. For general elections, I recoded open-seat status from zero to one if an incumbent suffered defeat in his primary (as indicated by the election results reported in the FEC data).

Freshman incumbent is a dummy variable for challengers only, coded one if the opposing incumbent has served only one term, zero otherwise. Freshmen incumbents for each cycle were identified using the FEC records from the previous cycle. *Retiring incumbent's party* is also a dummy variable, coded for open-seat candidates only, equaling one if the candidate belonged to the same party as the departing incumbent (as indicated by the previous cycle's FEC records), zero otherwise.

Party × year is a vector of dummy variables representing each combination of party and year. Each candidate's party is listed in a column of the FEC *cansum* files. The baseline category excluded from regressions is *Democrat—1992;* included categories are *Democrat—1994, Democrat—1996, Democrat—1998, Democrat—2000, Republican—1992, Republican—1994, Republican—1996, Republican—1998,* and *Republican—2000.* Some other variables are missing values for all cases in a particular year, so the dummies for those years also reflect the effects of the variables with missing values. For example, *previous nominee's margin* is unavailable for 1992 House candidates because all districts (except for at-large districts in Vermont, Alaska, Delaware, North Dakota, and South Dakota) had new boundaries after reapportionment and redistricting.

Normal party vote, calculated from the most recent presidential election returns for a candidate's state or district, equals each candidate's party's share of the two-party vote minus the national average for his or her party. Presidential results for each state and district were compiled from the *Almanac of American Politics.*

Pool of legislators, a control variable for equations using *experienced opponents* as the dependent variable, is the number of sitting state legislators from a candidate's party at the time of an election, as reported in the *Almanac of American Politics.*

To measure the strength and qualifications of candidates I (and, later, my research assistants) pored over back issues of *Congressional Quarterly Weekly Report* and the *Cook Political Report* and coded descriptions of candidate's backgrounds on the following dimensions: *previous elective office held, previous nonelective office held, other political activity, celebrity status, political family, employment sector, previous candidacy,* and *current officeholding status.* For candidates who were not mentioned in either of my two primary sources we conducted *Lexis-Nexis* searches. From these variables I constructed three of the variables used in the analysis. *Experienced candidate* is a dummy variable coded one if a candidate has been elected to any office at any level, zero otherwise. *Green & Krasno's candidate quality index* is a score that reflects variation within categories of elective experience based on candidates' elective experience, nonelective experience, other political activity, celebrity status, employment status, and previous runs for office (see Green and Krasno 1988, 888, for a description of the index).

Experienced opponents is the number of experienced opponents competing against any one candidate for a party nomination. *Out-party experienced opponents,* computed for open-seat candidates only, is the number of experienced candidates participating in the opposite party's primary.

I also used the *Cook Political Report* to code an a priori measure of House districts' competitiveness. The variable *Cook's forecast,* based on Charlie Cook's first rating of a district's competitiveness, ranges from −3 (solid for the opponent's party) to +3 (solid for the candidate's party).

Under the Ethics in Government Act, candidates for the U.S. House of Representatives are required to file a Financial Disclosure Statement with the House Clerk. Candidates disclose the source and actual amount of earned income in the filing year and the previous year. They also must report the range of value for unearned (investment) income and all assets other than the candidate's personal residence. Only the source of a spouse's earned income must be disclosed, not the amount. I used data from Form B of these statements to tally *candidate earned income* directly. I also used Form B to approximate the value of *candidate assets* and *candidate unearned income.*

The categories for assets and unearned income are quite broad and preclude precise estimates of candidates' wealth. Nonetheless one can compute a reasonably good indicator. I determined that any assets held at the time of the filing could be potentially converted to self-financing, as could income from the current year. (Income from the previous year would presumably be reported in current assets if it were still available to spend, so I did not count previous year income.) Because many candidates indicated assets and income in the largest, unbounded category I could not use the midpoint of each range to estimate the value of a particular entry. Instead I used the minimum possible value of each reported asset or income amount, summing these amounts to produced the variables *candidate assets* and *candidate unearned income.* These variables underestimate actual candidate wealth, both because of the coding methodology and the reporting exclusions of spousal income and personal residences. It may also *over*estimate the amount of wealth that can be converted to self-financing, since many assets are not liquid.

Annual income is the sum of candidate earned income and candidate unearned income.

Median household income and *geographic area* for each congressional district was reported in CensusCD from Geolytics, Inc.

One-way campaigning is the sum of amounts listed in Campaign Study Group data files for the categories *electronic advertising, direct mail,* and *other advertising.* (See appendix F for more detail about the component categories.) *Travel expenses, polling expenses, staff and volunteer expenses,* and *total expenditures* are values listed individually in the CSG data.

Extreme self-financers were defined as candidates whose maximum self-financing exceeded the threshold amount established by the Bipartisan Campaign Reform Act. That threshold is fixed at $350,000 for House elections and varies with state population in Senate elections. In Senate elections the threshold for extreme self-financers equals $300,000 plus $.08 times the state voting age population. Voting age population for each election cycle is reported in the FEC publication *The Record.*

The variable *coordinated expenditure limit,* used as a control in the analysis of party spending patterns, was collected from *The Record.*

Appendix B:
Least Squares and Poisson Regression

LEAST SQUARES REGRESSION MODELS assume that the dependent variable is unbounded, continuous, and distributed normally. In practice, this assumption is often relaxed and least squares is used for dependent variables that are bounded and even discrete, but are distributed approximately normally.

In chapter 3 I used *experienced opponents* as a dependent variable. A count variable ranging from 0 to 7, *experienced opponents* is neither unbounded nor continuous. This recommends against using the least squares model but does not necessarily rule it out. However, if one simply plots the observed probability distribution of the number of experienced candidates in each primary, it is quite obvious that Poisson is a much more appropriate model than least squares.[1] Figure B.1 clearly illustrates the congruity between the actual, observed distribution of experienced candidates and the Poisson distribution. The white columns represent the observed distribution of the number of experienced candidates in each primary and the dark columns represent the expected distribution, given an assumption that the number of experienced candidates is distributed Poisson around a mean of .70, which is the mean observed in the data.[2] A normal distribution with a mean of .70 and standard deviation of .71 (the value observed in the data), on which least squares regression is based,

---

1. I plot the number of experienced candidates in each primary instead of the number of experienced opponents to each candidate because within each primary the number of experienced opponents for each candidate is mutually dependent.

2. The variance of a Poisson variable is equal to its mean, and the variance in the number of experienced candidates per primary is .71.

grossly underestimates the probability of observing *no* experienced candidates and grossly overestimates the probability of observing a *negative* number of experienced candidates. Of course, one can never observe fewer than zero experienced candidates in a primary.

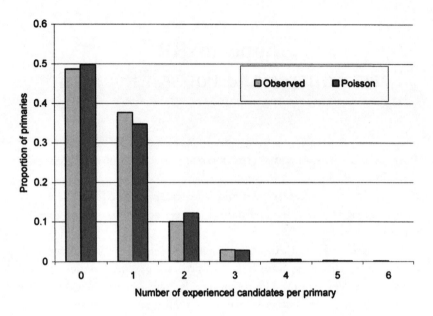

Fig. B.1.   Distribution of experienced candidates per potentially competitive primary and Poisson distribution

Appendix C:
Instrumental Variables and 2SLS

SCHOLARS HAVE LONG BEEN FRUSTRATED by the need to use instrumental variables when estimating the effect of campaign spending on election outcomes, as it has proven difficult to identify appropriate instruments for funding. For example, in 1978 Jacobson used *CP*, a dummy variable indicating whether the challenger or incumbent faced primary opposition, *YRS*, the number of consecutive years the incumbent has been in Congress, and *PO*, the now-familiar dichotomous measure of previous elective experience, as instruments for challenger spending. But subsequent scholars have dismissed all of these variables as inappropriate instruments for funding, since they all appear to have a direct impact on election outcomes (Abramowitz 1991; Gerber 1998; Goidel and Gross 1994; Green and Krasno 1988).

In appendix C of their 1988 article Green and Krasno propose "early receipts," defined as the total amount of funds received (from any source) through the postprimary report, as an instrumental variable for nonincumbent spending. Green and Krasno note:

> For "early receipts" ... to be considered a valid instrument, it is necessary to assume that early fund-raising goes on before any "firm" expectations may be formed based on [challenger vote share] itself. ...At a minimum, early receipts purge [challenger expenditures] of expectation-based surges in spending that may occur from late summer to election day (a period when over half of challenger money is spent). (1988, 904)

Gary Jacobson critiques this instrument: "Early receipts are just as subject to electoral expectations as later receipts, so they are also endogenous" (1990, 341). I find Jacobson's criticism unpersuasive. Early receipts may be subject to electoral expectations, but, as Green and Krasno suggest, electoral expectations in the off-year cannot possibly be as strongly related to the actual outcome as electoral expectations in the weeks immediately preceding an election. The closer the election, the better candidates can read their tea leaves. In fact, in my data set I found that *early contributions* were indeed correlated with *vote margin,* but the correlation was only .25. The correlation between *total contributions* and *vote margin* was .44. I therefore use *early contributions* as an instrumental variable for *total contributions.*

Appendix D: Why Diminishing Marginal Effects Should Be Modeled

As JACOBSON NOTES, "no candidate can get more than 100 percent of the vote, no matter how much is spent" (1978, 471). Once a candidate spends, say, $2 million, spending another $200,000 is not likely to sway anyone. So let us assume for the moment that funding indeed has a diminishing marginal effect on vote margin and that the effect does *not* depend on the mix of personal funds and raised contributions in the campaign treasury. For illustrative purposes let us also assume that the effect of funding on vote margin is proportional to the natural log of total funding, where total funding is the sum of *total self-financing* and *total contributions*.

$$E(\textit{vote margin}) = \beta_0 + \beta_1 \ln(\textit{total self-financing} + \textit{total contributions}) + XB$$

This relationship is depicted in figure D.1. As funding from any source increases, the marginal effect of funding decreases, as is also illustrated in figure D.1. One hundred thousand dollars improves a candidate's margin tremendously if that candidate has no other funds, but if the candidate already has $1 million, another $100,000 has much less impact.

Whether one self-finances $100 and raises $1 million or raises $100 and self-finances $1 million, the effect of funds totaling $1,000,100 is $\beta_1 \ln(1,000,100)$, or $13.8\beta_1$. In this model money is money is money and what matters is how much there is, not where it came from. This model of funding's effect on margins is source-neutral. Now I examine how this source-neutral dynamic would be realized in the real world of campaign finance by comparing two candidates, Sam Self-Financer and Frieda Fund-Raiser. Sam and Frieda are not actual candidates but I give them qualities

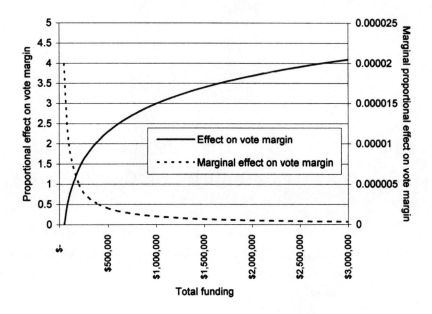

Fig. D.1. Representation of diminishing marginal effect of campaign funds on election results

that are representative of candidates in the real world, at least that part of it under consideration in this chapter.

Sam self-finances $100,000 and raises *total contributions*$_{Sam}$, so the effect of Sam's total funding is

$$\beta_1 \ln(100{,}000 + \textit{total contributions}_{Sam}).$$

If Sam did not self-finance at all, the effect of his funding would be

$$\beta_1 \ln(\textit{total contributions}_{Sam}),$$

so the *marginal* effect of Sam's $100,000 self-investment is

$$\beta_1 \ln(100{,}000 + \textit{total contributions}_{Sam}) - \beta_1 \ln(\textit{total contributions}_{Sam})$$

$$= \beta_1 \ln\left(\frac{\$100{,}000 + \textit{total contriubtions}_{Sam}}{\textit{total contributions}_{Sam}}\right)$$

$$= \beta_1 \ln\left(\frac{\$100{,}000}{\textit{total contributions}_{Sam}}\right).$$

The larger *total contributions*$_{Sam}$, the smaller the marginal effect of Sam's $100,000 self-investment. Similarly, if Frieda raises $100,000, the marginal effect of her contributions is

$$\beta_1 \ln\left(\frac{\$100,000}{total\ self\text{-}financing_{Frieda}} + 1\right).$$

As Frieda self-finances more, raising $100,000 helps her less.

Here is how Sam and Frieda resemble real-world candidates: Sam is the *average* candidate who self-finances $100,000, and Frieda happens to be the *average* candidate who raises $100,000. Linear regression indicates that among sampled nominees,

E(*Total contributions*) = $443,847 − .03626 × *Total self-financing*

and

E(*Total self-financing*) = $70,004 − .01147 × *Total contributions.*

Since Sam and Frieda are the average candidates who self-finance and raise $100,000, respectively, Sam raises $440,221 ($443,847 − .03626 × $100,000) and Frieda self-finances $68,858 ($70,004 − .01147 × $100,000). The marginal effect of Sam's $100,000 self-investment is $\beta_1\ln(100,000/440,221 + 1)$, or $.20\beta_1$ and the marginal effect of Frieda's $100,000 raised is $\beta_1\ln(100,000/68,858 + 1)$, or $.89\beta_1$. Frieda gets three-and-a-half times more bang for her buck with raised contributions than Sam does with personal funding, even though she raises the same amount—$100,000— as Sam self-finances (see figure D.2 for an illustration). This is not because fund-raising is inherently more productive than self-financing—the model itself is source-neutral. Rather, because candidates tend to raise more than they self-finance, the marginal effect of self-financing $100,000 is less than the marginal effect of raising $100,000.

This finding is not a function of the amount chosen, $100,000. In this data set, average *total funding* for any given level of *total self-financing* always exceeds average *total funding* given the same amount of *total contributions*. Neither is the functional form of the example, ln(*total self-financing* + *total contributions*), to blame. *Any* function for which the marginal effect decreases with total funding would produce a gap between the marginal effect of fund-raising and the marginal effect of self-financing.

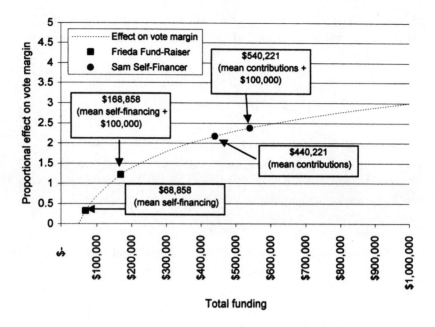

Fig. D.2.   Comparing Sam Self-Financer and Frieda Fund-Raiser

Appendix E: Approximating the Rate of Diminishing Marginal Effects

IN THE CASE OF CAMPAIGN FUNDING there is good reason to believe that the scale on which the variable is measured, dollars, does not correspond linearly to the property of the variable in which I am interested, its power to sway voters. Ignoring this incongruence can lead to misleading statistical results.

William Jacoby suggests that, as a way of dealing with this problem, "numeric values assigned to . . . observations can also be regarded as parameters to be estimated during the course of the analysis" (1999, 280). Jacoby estimates these parameters using goodness-of-fit statistics, choosing the transformation of X that produces the best fit between the data and the model.

Unfortunately, two-stage least squares with instrumental variables does not produce a meaningful goodness-of-fit statistic. Some software packages report an R^2 statistic, but R^2 does *not* indicate goodness of fit in 2SLS as it does in OLS (Sribney and Wiggins 1999). In fact, because 2SLS is a method for estimating structural parameters (i.e., slope coefficients) in models that are not fully specified, there is no meaningful goodness-of-fit statistic for 2SLS. I was consequently unable to use Jacoby's method for determining the transformation of funding variables that would best capture the actual, nonlinear effect of funding on vote margins.

As an alternative, I did the following in the spirit of Jacoby's recommendation. I began by performing a first-stage regression of *funding* (or *self-financing* plus *contributions*) on the independent variables in the model of *vote margin* and the instrumental variables. I saved the predicted values and also created several dummy variables, each representing a range of *predicted funding*. For example, in the sample of challengers the dummy variables represented increments of $50,000—zero to $50,000, $50,000 to $100,000, $100,000 to $150,000, and so on. In the second stage regression, I included *predicted funding,* the dummy variables and interaction terms for *predicted funding* and each dummy variable.[1] Within each of the four samples of nominees, I then used the Box-Cox procedure to find the transformation of *predicted funding* that best matched the *predicted effect of funding.* A Box-Cox transformation takes the form:

$$\frac{(total\ self\text{-}financing\ +\ total\ contributions)^{\lambda} - 1}{\lambda}.$$

For all four samples the value of λ that produced the transformation of *predicted funding* that best matched the *predicted effect of funding* was close to .5. Because these values are only approximations, I set λ equal to .5 for all four samples to make the coefficient estimates comparable across equations.

---

1. Because this procedure used a large number of degrees of freedom—12 or 14 depending on the sample—and because the variance in most of the *funding* variables was quite small, the standard errors of the coefficient estimates were all quite large. I therefore could not draw any strong statistical conclusions directly from the coefficient estimates.

Appendix F: Campaign Spending Data

I ACQUIRED A DATA SET of campaign expenditures from the Campaign Study Group, which describes itself as "a for-profit consulting firm specializing in campaign finance research and public opinion analysis" (Campaign Study Group 2000). The data include the amount spent by each candidate in 28 different categories. The labels for each category, along with a description of the five categories I use in chapter 5, are copied from the appendix of *Gold-Plated Politics* (Fritz and Morris 1992), a volume coauthored by CSG's president.

Overhead
Office furniture/supplies
Rent/utilities
Salaries
Taxes
Bank/investment fees
Lawyers/accountants
Telephone
Campaign automobile
Computers/office equipment
Travel
Food/meetings
Fund-Raising
Events
Direct mail
Telemarketing
Polling

Advertising
Electronic media
Other media
Other Campaign Activity
Actual campaigning
Persuasion mail/brochures
Staff/Volunteers
Unidentified Actual Campaigning
Constituent Gifts/Entertainment
Donations
Candidates from same state
Candidates from other states
Civic organizations
Ideological groups
Political parties
Unitemized Expense

Electronic media. All payments to consultants, separate purchases of broadcast time, and production costs associated with the development of radio and television advertising. In most cases, payments to media consultants for other purposes were excluded.

Other media. Payments for billboards; advertising in newspapers, journals, magazines, and publications targeted to religious groups, senior citizens, and other special constituencies; as well as program ads purchased from local charitable and booster organizations.

Direct mail. All costs associated with the strictly promotional mailings undertaken by campaigns, including artwork, printing of the brochures or other mailed material, postage, the purchase of mailing lists, as well as consultant fees and consultant expenses.

Staff/volunteers. All food expenses for staff and volunteers, including phone bank and get-out-the-vote volunteers. These expenses included bottled water, soda machines, monthly coffee service, and food purchases that were specifically for the campaign office. Also included were recruitment of volunteers, gifts for staff and volunteers, and staff retreats.

Travel. All general travel expenses, such as airfare and hotels, as well as rental cars, taxis, daily parking, and entries such as "food for travel."

Polling. All polling costs, including payments to consultants as well as in-kind contributions of polling results to the campaign.

I purchased data for 1994. The Campaign Study Group offered to sell me data for 1992 as well, but after I inspected the 1994 data I decided not to purchase additional years because I was concerned about significant measurement error. Specifically, I found notable discrepancies between the amount of total spending reported by CSG and a close approximation of expenditures calculated from the FEC data files. Unfortunately, the FEC *cansum* data files do *not* consistently include entries for contribution refunds, so I cannot exclude these amounts from my calculation of expenditures from the FEC data. (CSG rightly does not classify contribution refunds as expenditures.) Still, the differences between CSG and FEC data were too large to be attributed to this discrepancy. The correlation between expenditures reported by CSG and expenditures reported by the FEC is .68 for incumbents, .38 for challengers and only .07 for open-seat candidates. The two measures differed by an average of $201,471 for incumbents, $425,519 for open-seat candidates, and $196,331 for challengers.

I wrote to CSG President Dwight Morris to express my concern. Morris replied, "Our numbers will usually not match the FEC numbers" and explained that CSG actually corrects errors that candidates make on their reports. So, for example, Morris explained that "we sometimes have to include money listed as transfers to other authorized committees but which is actually contributions to other campaigns and party committees" (Morris 2000). (I subtract the amount reported as transfers to authorized committees from my calculation of expenditures because shifting money around from one committee to another is clearly not campaign spending and would not be itemized by CSG.)

I remain skeptical. Some of the difference between CSG's measures and my approximations are certainly attributable to CSG's corrections and to the inclusion of contribution refunds, but it seems improbable that the legitimate differences are so large that there was no substantive or statistical correlation between the two measures of expenditures among open-seat candidates.

The open-seat data are clearly problematic, so I do not consider the spending patterns of open-seat candidates in chapter 5. However, I do use the data for challengers. The correlation between the CSG and FEC measures of total expenditures, .38, is highly significant ($p < .001$). So while there may be measurement error, the CSG measures certainly do reflect actual patterns of spending. One should remember that random error in a dependent variable does *not* bias regression coefficient estimates, so unless there is some systematic under- or overmeasurement of certain kinds of expenditures, the relationships I identified in chapter 5 are valid.

References

Abramowitz, Alan I. 1991. Incumbency, Campaign Spending, and the Decline of Competition in U.S. Elections. *Journal of Politics* 53 (1): 34–56.

Adamany, David W., and George E. Agree. 1975. *Political Money: A Strategy for Campaign Financing in America*. Baltimore: Johns Hopkins University Press.

Alexander, Herbert E. 1986. Financing Congressional Campaigns: Contributors, PACs, and Parties. In *Hearings on S. 59, S. 1072, S. 1563, S. 1787, S. 1806, S. 1891, and S. 2016, Proposed Amendments to the Federal Election Campaign Act of 1971*. United States Senate. 99th Cong., 2d sess., Serial No. 61-309 O.

Associated Press. 2000. *NJ Voters Unconcerned about Corzine's Spending Record,* June 18, 2000. Available from http://www.newsday.com (accessed June 18, 2000).

Banks, Jeffrey S., and D. Roderick Kiewiet. 1989. Explaining Patterns of Candidate Competition in Congressional Elections. *American Journal of Political Science* 33 (4): 997–1015.

Beard, Charles A. [1957] 1987. Framing the Constitution. In *American Government: Readings and Cases,* edited by P. Woll. Boston: Little, Brown. Original edition, Charles A. Beard, 1957, *The Economic Basis of Politics and Related Writings by Charles A. Beard*.

Bianco, William T. 1984. Strategic Decisions on Candidacy in U.S. Congressional Districts. *Legislative Studies Quarterly* 9 (2): 351–64.

Biersack, Robert, Paul S. Herrnson, and Clyde Wilcox. 1993. Seeds for Success: Early Money in Congressional Elections. *Legislative Studies Quarterly* 18 (4): 535–51.

Black, Chris. 1992. Clinton: America Needs a "Mother's Love." *Boston Globe,* May 11, 8.

Black, Gordon. 1972. A Theory of Political Ambition: Career Choices and the Role of Structural Incentives. *American Political Science Review* 66 (1): 144–59.

Blitzer, Wolf, Brent Sadler, Jeanne Meserve, Susan Page, Steve Roberts, Tucker Carlson, and Bruce Morton. 2000. Syrian President Hafez Al-Assad Dead at 69; Campaign Finance Questions Re-Emerge. In *CNN Late Edition with Wolf Blitzer,* Lexis-Nexis Academic Universe.

Bloom, Joel David. 1998. Kerrey's Millionaires: The DSCC and Candidates Recruitment in 1996. Paper presented at the annual meeting of the Western Political Science Association, Los Angeles.

Bond, Jon R., Cary Covington, and Richard Fleisher. 1985. Explaining Challenger Quality in Congressional Elections. *Journal of Politics* 47 (2): 510–29.

Buckley, Frank. 2000. Can the Power of Money Make the Difference in the New York Senate Primary? In *CNN The World Today,* Lexis-Nexis Academic Universe.

Cain, Bruce E. 1995. Lessons from the Inside Revisited. In *The 1994 Governor's Race,* edited by G. C. Lubenow. Berkeley, Calif.: Institute of Governmental Studies Press.

Cain, Bruce E., John A. Ferejohn, and Morris P. Fiorina. 1987. *The Personal Vote: Constituency Service and Electoral Independence.* Cambridge: Harvard University Press.

Canon, David T. 1990. *Actors, Athletes, and Astronauts: Political Amateurs in the United States Congress.* Chicago: University of Chicago Press.

———. 1993. Sacrificial Lambs or Strategic Politicians? Political Amateurs in U.S. House Elections. *American Journal of Political Science* 37 (4): 1119–41.

CensusCD. 1996. CD-ROM. Geolytics, Inc.

Cross, Al. 1998. Campaign Money Keeps Center Stage in Senate Race: Baesler, Henry Amass Debts Trying to Catch Up to Owen. *Courier-Journal,* May 25, 1B.

Crotty, William J. 1977. *Political Reform and the American Experiment.* New York: Thomas Y. Crowell.

Dahl, Robert A. 1956. *A Preface to Democratic Theory.* Chicago: University of Chicago Press.

FEC (Federal Election Commission). 1998. Advisory Opinion 1997–21. April 20.

Fenno, Richard F., Jr. 1978. *Home Style: House Members in Their Districts.* New York: Harper-Collins.

Fritz, Sara. 2000. It Takes More Than Money to Win an Election. *New York Times,* May 29, 4A.

Fritz, Sara, and Dwight Morris. 1992. *Gold-Plated Politics: Running for Congress in the 1990s.* Washington, D.C.: Congressional Quarterly.

Gerber, Alan. 1998. Estimating the Effect of Campaign Spending on Senate Election Outcomes using Instrumental Variables. *American Political Science Review* 92 (2): 401–12.

Goidel, Robert K., and Donald A. Gross. 1994. A Systems Approach to Campaign Finance in U.S. House Elections. *American Politics Quarterly* 22 (2): 125–53.

Goodliffe, Jay 2001. The Effect of War Chests on Challenger Entry in US House Elections. *American Journal of Political Science* 45 (4): 830–44.

Green, Donald Philip, and Jonathan S. Krasno. 1988. Salvation for the Spendthrift Incumbent: Reestimating the Effects of Campaign Spending in House Elections. *American Journal of Political Science* 32 (4): 884–907.

———. 1990. Rebuttal to Jacobson's "New Evidence of Old Arguments." *American Journal of Political Science* 34 (2): 363–72.

Halbfinger, David M. 2000. Corzine's Ties to Goldman Sachs Could Become a Political Liability. *New York Times,* May 6, B1.

Halbfinger, David M., and Marjorie Connelly. 2000. Poll Finds Corzine Spending Is Not a Problem for Voters. *New York Times,* October 18, B1.

Hamburger, Tom. 2000. Who Wants a Multi-Millionaire? Democrats, to Help Win Senate. *Wall Street Journal,* October 19, A28.

Harpaz, Beth J. 1998. Big Task Lies Ahead for Schumer. *Buffalo News,* November 22, 1A.

Harshbarger, Scott. 2001. *Statement of Common Cause President Scott Harshbarger on "Millionaires' Amendment" to McCain-Feingold.* Press release. Common Cause, March 20, 2001. Available from http://www.commoncause.org/publications/march01/032001st.htm (accessed June 8, 2004).

Helm, Theo. 2004. Broyhill's Contributions Invoke "Millionaires' Amendment." *Winston-Salem Journal,* June 15, B1.

Herrnson, Paul S. 1995. *Congressional Elections: Campaigning at Home and in Washington.* Washington, D.C.: CQ Press.

———. 2000. *Congressional Elections: Campaigning at Home and in Washington.* Washington, D.C.: CQ Press.

Jacobs, Andrew. 2000. In Bayonne, Blue-Collar Backlash over Corzine's Spending. *New York Times,* May 30, B1.

Jacobson, Gary C. 1975. The Impact of Broadcast Campaigning on Electoral Outcomes. *Journal of Politics* 37 (3): 769–93.

———. 1978. The Effects of Campaign Spending in Congressional Elections. *American Political Science Review* 72 (2): 469–91.

———. 1980. *Money in Congressional Elections.* New Haven: Yale University Press.

———. 1985. Money and Votes Reconsidered: Congressional Elections, 1972–1982. *Public Choice* 47 (1): 7–62.

———. 1989. Strategic Politicians and the Dynamics of House Elections, 1946–86. *American Political Science Review* 83 (3): 773–93.

———. 1990. The Effects of Campaigning in House Elections: New Evidence for Old Arguments. *American Journal of Political Science* 34 (2): 334–62.

———. 1997. *The Politics of Congressional Elections.* New York: Addison-Wesley.

Jacobson, Gary C., and Samuel Kernell. [1981] 1983. *Strategy and Choice in Congressional Elections.* Binghamton, N.Y.: Vail-Ballou Press.

Jacoby, William G. 1999. Levels of Measurement and Political Research: An Optimistic View. *American Journal of Political Science* 43 (1): 271–301.

Johnson, Kirk. 2004. Senate Beckons a Coors from Beer to Political Ads. *New York Times,* April 24, A11.

Keller, Amy, and Mark Preston. 2001. Senators Tackle Cantwell Debt. *Roll Call,* March 26.

Kenny, Christopher, and Michael McBurnett. 1994. An Individual Level Multiequation Model of Expenditure Effects in Contested House Elections. *American Political Science Review* 88 (3): 669–707.

Kolodny, Robin A. 1998. *Pursuing Majorities.* Norman: University of Oklahoma Press.

Krasno, Jonathan S. 1994. *Challengers, Competition, and Reelection: Comparing Senate and House Elections.* New Haven: Yale University Press.

Krasno, Jonathan S., and Donald Philip Green. 1988. Preempting Quality Challengers in House Elections. *Journal of Politics* 50 (4): 920–36.

Kurtz, Josh. 2004. Oxford Trips Millionaire Amendment in Primary. *Roll Call,* July 6.

Los Angeles Times. 1985. 2 Formulas Bring End to "Coke Is It" Campaign. September 13, 4.

Lubenow, Gerald C., ed. 1995. *The 1994 Governor's Race.* Berkeley, Calif.: Institute of Governmental Studies Press.

———, ed. 1999. *California Votes: The 1998 Governor's Race.* Berkeley, Calif.: Institute of Governmental Studies Press.

Maisel, Louis Sandy. [1982] 1986. *From Obscurity to Oblivion.* Knoxville: University of Tennessee Press.

Mann, Thomas E., and Raymond E. Wolfinger. 1981. Candidates and Parties in Congressional Elections. *American Political Science Review* 74 (3): 617–32.

Mayhew, David R. 1974. *Congress: The Electoral Connection.* New Haven: Yale University Press.

Miller, Alan C., and Dwight Morris. 1992. Congressional Hopeful Sets Campaign Spending Record. *New York Times,* October 28, A1.

Milyo, Jeffrey, and Timothy Groseclose. 1999. The Electoral Effects of Incumbent Wealth. *Journal of Law and Economics* 42 (2): 699–722.

Morris, Dwight L. 2000. E-mail message to Jennifer Steen. January 6.

New York Times. 1996. The Power of Rich Candidates. February 29, A20.

Pike, John. 1996. The Force Is With Her: The Cold War's Over, but Star Wars Funds Are Sky-High. *Mother Jones,* September–October.

Pitkin, Hanna Fenichel. 1967. *The Concept of Representation.* Berkeley: University of California Press.

Postman, David. 2000. Cantwell to Turn Down PAC Cash in Senate Bid. *New York Times,* May 5, B1.

Public Policy Institute of California. 1998. PPIC Statewide Survey: The Changing Political Landscape of California.

Sanko, John, and John Brinkley. 1997. Romer Robs State of Great Race. *Rocky Mountain News,* September 27, 6A.

Schumpeter, Joseph A. [1942] 1947. *Capitalism, Socialism, and Democracy.* New York: Harper and Brothers.

Sher, Andy, Lisa LaPolt, and Jeff Woods. 1996. Running for Office? Don't Forget to Stop By the Bank. *Nashville Banner,* February 9, B1.

Simon, Mark. 2000. Muscle Flex Pays Off for Honda: Campbell's Seat Seen as "In Play" by Democrats. *San Francisco Chronicle,* March 9.

Smith, Richard A. 1995. Interest Group Influence in the U.S. Congress. *Legislative Studies Quarterly* 20 (1): 89–139.

Sorauf, Frank J. 1992. *Inside Campaign Finance: Myths and Realities.* New Haven: Yale University Press.

Squire, Peverill. 1989. Challengers in U.S. Senate Elections. *Legislative Studies Quarterly* 14 (4): 531–47.

Sribney, William, and Vince Wiggins. 1999. "Missing R-squared for 2SLS/IV." *Frequently Asked Questions.* StataCorp. Available at http://www.stata.com/support/faqs/stat/2sls .html.

Steen, Jennifer A. 1997. Candidate Quality: Issues of Conceptualization and Measurement. Typescript. Available at http://www2.bc.edu/~steenje/2004/PO719/239.pdf.

―――. 1999. Money Doesn't Grow on Trees: Fundraising in American Political Campaigns. In *Handbook of Political Marketing,* edited by B. I. Newman. Thousand Oaks, Calif.: Sage Publications.

―――. 2003a. The Millionaires' Amendment. In *Life After Reform: When the BCRA Meets Politics,* edited by M. Malbin. Lanham, Md.: Rowman and Littlefield.

―――. 2003b. Trickle-Up Competition: State Term Limits and Candidate Emergence in Congressional Elections. Paper presented at the annual meeting of the Midwest Political Science Association, April, Chicago.

―――. 2006. Self-Financed Candidates and the "Millionaires' Amendment." In *The Election After Reform: Money, Politics and the Bipartisan Campaign Reform Act,* edited by M. Malbin. Lanham, Md.: Rowman and Littlefield.

Stone, Walter J. 1999. E-mail message to Jennifer Steen. July 8.

Stone, Walter J., Louis Sandy Maisel, Cherie Maestas, and Sean Evans. 1998. A New Perspective on Candidate Quality in U.S. House Elections. Paper presented at the annual meeting of the Midwest Political Science Association, Chicago.

Todd, Charles. 1997. *'98 House Races: Open Seat Contests.* NationalJournal.com, September 16, 1997. Available from http://nationaljournal.com/members/buzz/1997/trail/091697.htm (accessed September 23, 2003).

———. 2000. *New Economy Politics.* NationalJournal.com, May 31, 2000. Available from http://nationaljournal.com/members/buzz/2000/trail/053100.htm (accessed September 23, 2003).

U.S. House. 2002a. Rep. Shelley Moore Capito speaking on Bipartisan Campaign Reform Act of 2001. *Congressional Record.* 107th Cong., 2d sess. Vol. 148, no. 13, daily edition (February 13): H430.

U.S. House. 2002b. Rep. Tom Davis speaking on Bipartisan Campaign Reform Act of 2001. *Congressional Record.* 107th Cong., 2d sess. Vol. 148, no. 13, daily edition (February 13): H431.

U.S. Senate. 1971. Committee on Commerce. Subcommittee on Communications. Hearings on S.1, S.382, and S.956, Federal Election Campaign Act of 1971. 92d Cong., 1st sess. Washington, D.C.: GPO.

U.S. Senate. 1987a. Sen. Dennis DeConcini speaking on Senatorial Election Campaign Act. *Congressional Record.* 100th Cong., 1st sess. Vol. 133, no. 90, daily edition (June 4): S7651.

U.S. Senate. 1987b. Sen. Pete Domenici speaking on Limited Candidate Expenditures of Personal Funds. *Congressional Record.* 100th Cong., 1st sess. Vol. 133, no. 32, daily edition (March 3): S2685.

U.S. Senate. 2001a. Sen. Robert Bennett speaking on Bipartisan Campaign Reform Act of 2001. *Congressional Record.* 107th Cong., 1st sess. Vol. 147, no. 36, daily edition (March 19): S2453.

U.S. Senate. 2001b. Sen. Susan Collins speaking on Bipartisan Campaign Reform Act of 2001. *Congressional Record.* 107th Cong., 1st sess. Vol. 147, no. 36, daily edition (March 19): S2469.

U.S. Senate. 2001c. Sen. Mike DeWine speaking on Bipartisan Campaign Reform Act of 2001. *Congressional Record.* 107th Cong., 1st sess. Vol. 147, no. 37, daily edition (March 20): S2539.

U.S. Senate. 2001d. Sen. Christopher Dodd speaking on Bipartisan Campaign Reform Act of 2001. *Congressional Record.* 107th Cong., 1st sess. Vol. 147, no. 37, daily edition (March 20): S2540.

U.S. Senate. 2001e. Sen. Dick Durbin speaking on Bipartisan Campaign Reform Act of 2001. *Congressional Record.* 107th Cong., 1st sess. Vol. 147, no. 37, daily edition (March 20): S2540.

U.S. Senate. 2001f. Sen. Jeff Sessions speaking on Bipartisan Campaign Reform Act of 2001. *Congressional Record.* 107th Cong., 1st sess. Vol. 147, no. 36, daily edition (March 19): S2464.

Van Biema, David. 1994. What Money Can Buy. *Time,* June 20, 35.

Walsh, Kenneth T. 1996. The Gilded Age of American Politics. *U.S. News and World Report,* May 20, 26.

Washingtonpost.com. 1998. Dwight Morris and the Campaign Study Group. Available at http://www.washingtonpost.com/wp-srv/politics/campaigns/money/writer.htm (accessed May 21, 2005).

Welch, W. P. 1981. Money and Votes: A Simultaneous Equation Model. *Public Choice* 36 (2): 209–34.

Wilcox, Clyde. 1988. I Owe It All to Me: Candidates' Investments in Their Own Campaigns. *American Politics Quarterly* 16:266–79.

Wilgoren, Jodi. 2003. Illinois Senator Announces He Won't Seek Re-election. *New York Times,* April 15, A1.

Index